KANSAS MATTERS:
America's Social Faultlines

Mark E. McCormick

BLUE
CEDAR
PRESS

"*Kansas Matters* sits at the intersection of journalism and moral inquiry. Mark McCormick draws on personal experience, original reporting and lessons of history to explore race, power and belonging. He reveals how one state's struggles mirror the nation's, showing who we've been but also who we may yet become."
Polly Bashore Wenzl, former Russian correspondent and newspaper editor, philanhropist, and author

"*Kansas Matters: America's Social Faultlines* serves as a comprehensive guide to the historical and contemporary trajectories of Kansas and the broader national social and political landscape. In this insightful work, Mark McCormick presents his multifaceted history and a profound sense of shared struggle that unites him with the world. Through eloquent and thoughtful prose, McCormick offers a compelling analysis of our past as Kansas and as a nation, as well as our future prospects."
Shawn Leigh Alexander, Ph.D., author of *An Army of Lions: The Civil Rights Struggle before the NAACP*, professor and Chair of African and African American Studies and Director of the Langston Hughes Center University of Kansas.

Table of Contents

PREFACE

Kansas is often overlooked, yet it has been a crucible for American transformation and the setting for diametrically opposed movements.

It was a major escape route for those fleeing enslavement and Kansans fought over whether to be a free or a slave state for ten years, a precursor to the U.S. Civil War. In 1879, 40,000 freed Black southerners moved to Kansas to escape growing violence.

In 1881, Kansas was the first state to enact Prohibition laws. Carrie Nation was a Kansan!

In 1887, Kansas was the first state to elect a woman mayor.

In the 1890s, leaders of the Populist movement — one of the largest third-party movements in U.S. history — included Kansans Mary Elizabeth Lease, Annie Diggs, and "Sockless Jerry" Simpson.

Kansas Black communities shaped the Harlem Renaissance. *The Appeal to Reason*, the largest socialist newspaper in the United States, came out of Girard, Kansas from 1895-1922, and published over a thousand titles of inexpensive paperback books, called Little Blue Books, classic fiction and nonfiction for ordinary people.

Pioneering Progressive journalist, William Allen White, ran as an independent for governor in 1924 because two candidates had been endorsed by the Ku Klux Klan. That year the Klan's Imperial Convocation in Kansas drew 5,000 people, and 43 people were lynched in the state.

In 1954, Oliver Brown, a Black pastor in Topeka, Kansas, gave his name to the landmark *Brown v. Board of Education* school desegregation decision.

Kansans in Wichita launched the earliest successful student-led civil rights sit-ins of the modern civil rights movement in the summer of 1958, eighteen months before sit-ins began in the South. Decades later, in 1991, "Summer of Mercy" anti-abortion protests began drawing national attention, and in 2009, an anti-abortion activist entered Sunday service at a Wichita Lutheran church and murdered local doctor George Tiller for performing abortions.

In contrast, Lawrence, Kansas passed one of the nation's first gay rights ordinances in 1995.

And in 2022, Kansas was the first state to take to the voters a referendum on abortion rights. The voters affirmed the state constitution's *protection of reproductive rights* in spite of and against the U.S. Supreme Court's *Dobbs* decision. *Dobbs v. Jackson* had months earlier overturned *Roe v Wade* and removed the constitutional right to abortion.

In all of this Kansas has mattered. The struggles taking place in this fly over state of America's Great Plains have always mattered. They have consistently driven national conversations.

This book collects recent columns by prize-winning journalist Mark E. McCormick that report how people in Kansas are experiencing these larger currents. It looks first at progress that is being erased since 2024. Then, it spotlights individuals who challenge the status quo for a more compassionate way of treating their neighbors. Finally, these short pieces explore important, less familiar issues that matter greatly to our nation's future, issues that are playing out now in Kansas.

The Board of Blue Cedar Press

April 2026

ERASURE?

1/ Kansas: The "Historically" Indispensable State

Think about this.

A monument in Selma, Alabama, honors the Rev. James Reeb, among others in the civil rights movement. (Mark McCormick)

The 2012 Oscar-winning film *Lincoln*, featuring Daniel Day Lewis, opened with a conversation between Lincoln and two soldiers from the Second Kansas Colored Regiment.

Kansans played a critical role in the establishment of the Smithsonian's National Museum of African American History and Culture. Then Senator Sam Brownback brought the bill in the Senate to establish the museum. The late civil rights icon Rep. John Lewis brought a similar bill in the House.

President George W. Bush appointed my friend Eric Sexton to the charter board for the museum, and Kansas had more people on that board than any other state.

Inside the museum, Kansas history resounds.

A Stearman plane, most likely built in Wichita, hangs from the ceiling. There's a Nicodemus sign featured in an exhibition about Black towns. The Topeka *Brown v. Board* decision is featured in the segregation section, along with items my staff at the Kansas African American Museum submitted about the 1958 Dockum sit-in, the first successful student-led sit-in in the nation's history.

There's also art from Topeka's Aaron Douglass, references to John Brown and "Bleeding Kansas," images of native Wichitan Hattie McDaniel — the first Black person to win an Oscar — and photographs of and by the great Gordon Parks, a native of Fort Scott.

Others seem to value our history more than we do.

A few years ago, while I still worked at the Kansas African American Museum, some historians reached out from the U.N. Educational, Scientific and Cultural Organization, also known as UNESCO. They discussed establishing Topeka as "the western terminus" of an American Civil Rights Trail.

All this, and we've only scratched the surface.

In northeast Kansas, we could have an anchor museum in Quindaro, considered the first and best example of a multi-racial democracy in Kansas or elsewhere. A walking path from Quindaro could simulate the Underground Railroad all the way to Topeka.

In south-central Kansas, there should be a President Barack Obama heritage site because his mom was born there; a larger "Double V" Campaign memorial; and preservation of the old St. Peter Claver Catholic Church, where Dockum sit-in participants practiced and steeled themselves for their step into history.

We also could expand the Kansas African American History Trail. The original trail was launched by Nicodemus native Angela Bates. Back when I was at the Kansas African American Museum, we wrote a federal grant adding signage that directed tourists to sites across the state, including the Buffalo Soldier Monument in Leavenworth, the Ritchie House in Topeka and a John Brown site in Osawatomie.

All this, and we still haven't brushed on Donald Hollowell, born in Wichita but known in Atlanta as "Mr. Civil Rights" for serving clients such as King, John Lewis and Julian Bond, and for giving Washington, D.C., power broker Vernon Jordan his first job.

Other states would cherish these kinds of historical and cultural opportunities. To whom much is given, much is required, right?

Just because we have history to spare, doesn't mean that we should.

2/ Whitewashing History: Malcolm to Nikole

Published in *Blue Angel Landing Journal*,
Volume III

Here, in the pretend innocence of middle America, we could not expect much truth about anything historical. Here, on land seized from people who'd been seized and marched here from the American Southeast, the dominant culture prefers nostalgia to history.

So, in school, teachers told of slave traders and slaveowners, while hiding perhaps slavery's most brutal aspect – slave making. Ishmael Reed called them "nigger breakers." I learned of this in my early 20s from a slight book of 80-some pages, five pages of which roared with more terror than I'd ever confronted.

"They used to take a Black woman who would be pregnant," Malcolm X wrote in that book, "and tie her up by her toes, let her be hanging head down, and they would take a knife and cut her stomach open, let that Black, unborn child fall out, and then stomp its head in the ground." This was done, he said, in front of the husband/father, to breed such fear into the captives that no thought of rebellion would bloom in even the recesses of their minds.

"I'll show you the books where they write about this," Malcolm said. *"The American Slave-Trade: An Account of Its Origin, Growth, and Suppression* by John R. Spears; *From Slavery to Freedom* by John Hope Franklin, *Negro Family in the U.S.* by

E. Franklin Frazier, ... *Anti-Slavery,* by Dwight Lowell Drummond. "

The book, *Malcolm X on Afro-American History*, was published in 1967, the year I was born.

Just two years ago, I met Nikole Hannah-Jones, to whom Malcolm the firebrand passed his torch that lit the path forward and also kindled 400-plus years of tortured anger. Her fires have threatened the fragile nostalgia that gauzes our ears and eyelids. Senators have taken to a kind of aerial firefighting, blanketing the culture in foamy retardants to prevent the lies from being burned away:

White Supremacy/Racism predates our national origin; We developed sharp-pencil accounting to drive greater productivity from human beings; George Washington didn't have wooden teeth, his teeth were not even his, they were ripped from unwilling mouths.

"It's actually simple," Hannah-Jones said, "If you can feel pride in things you didn't personally take part in, you can feel shame in things you didn't personally take part in. Some of you are motivated to make this hard, but it's only hard because you want the glory of our history but not the burden."

1776 doesn't explain January 6th, she said. But 1619 does.

3/ Upset about Diversity? Revisit your History

February 5, 2025

A nifty little book, *From the Browder File*, explains the origin of the word "negro." Anthony Browder, the book's author, said the word emanated from a cultural misunderstanding.

"When the Greeks traveled to Africa 2,500 years ago, the Egyptian civilization was already ancient," Browder wrote. "The Great Pyramid was over 3,000 years old, and the sphinx was even older. Writing, science, medicine and religion were already a part of the civilization that had reached its zenith."

The Greeks came to learn, he said, but certain nuances escaped visitors who mistook the reverence of ancestors for worship of the dead. Browder said the word "negro" is Spanish for black, and that the Spanish language comes from Latin, which has its origins in Classical Greek. The word "negro" in Greek is derived from the root word "necro," meaning dead, as in "necromancy" or communication with the dead, or so-called "black magic."

"When the Greeks returned to Europe," Browder wrote, "they took their distorted beliefs with them and the word negro evolved out of this great misunderstanding."

In similar ways, a tragic confusion about the Black experience continues to this day in the United States, spreading the viruses of ignorance and racism. Misunderstanding feeds misperceptions of diversity efforts designed to address the ongoing hurt born from our racial caste system.

It will not be until 2289 that Black people on this continent will have been free as long as they had been subject to slavery and segregation. And that takes us from 1619 to 1954's *Brown v. Board* decision. No one thinks things were great then for Black people in 1954.

This nation used racial privilege as one of its organizing ideas, and we're still living with it.

Despite this, on his first day in office, President Donald Trump signed an executive order killing diversity, equity, inclusion and accessibility mandates, policies, programs, preferences and activities in "the Federal Government, under whatever name they appear."

The next day, he rescinded numerous executive actions of past administrations. Neither he nor the people cheering these executive orders know about or fully acknowledge why such programs remain necessary.

The claim is that these policies discriminate against white Americans, but how could this be true when white women and by extension, white families, were the primary beneficiaries of affirmative action and DEI policies?

A May 2023 article in *Forbes Magazine* written by Michelle Penelope King, a "gender equity expert," said "while many white women have made gains in American workplaces, the gains for racial and ethnic minority women haven't been as significant."

King cited a study saying white women held nearly 19% of all C-suite positions, while racial and ethnic minority women only hold 4%.

"Overall, white women have benefitted disproportionally from corporate DEI efforts," King wrote.

These programs existed because the people who for years lectured Black America about "personal responsibility" have yet to accept their responsibility for perpetuating the practices making DEI programs necessary.

In our society, the mere feelings of white people matter more than the lived experiences of nonwhite people.

White people feel they suffered reverse discrimination, and the president issued a raft of executive orders. White students feel uncomfortable hearing about what happened to Black and Indigenous people, and books got banned and teachers and librarians got fired.

The actual grievances of Black and indigenous people? Ignored.

But comedian Jon Stewart said it best: If people are tired of *hearing* about racism, just imagine what it's like living under it. The upper caste's failure to honestly confront our history has led us to this point. Fixing it remains the only way out.

The noted historian John Hope Franklin, in an April 3, 1969, speech — the first Martin Luther King Jr. Lecture at The New School for Social Research — made precisely this argument about our education system.

"Indeed, [African Americans'] inferior position in American life could be maintained only if the fiction of them as a people with no history worth telling could be maintained," he said.

Franklin continued: "This is the history that has been written, and this is the kind of history that has been taught in our schools and colleges. It is uninformed, arrogant, uncharitable, undemocratic, and racist history."

Nearly 56 years later, Franklin's remarks seem eerily precise: "It has thus spawned and perpetrated an ignorant, self-seeking, super-patriotic, ethnocentric group of white Americans, who can say in this day and time that they did not know that Negroes had a history."

The antidote?

"We must rid ourselves of the spurious and specious teachings of the past," he wrote. "And in its place, we must teach a history that recognizes the worth of all people who have worked and died to make this country, whatever it is today."

Understood.

4/ Quindaro: The Vision

Previously published in a longer version by the ACLU Kansas

On a quiet bend of the Kansas River, up a lush tree- and rock-covered slope, a Kansas that should have been, slumbers.

Enslaved people fleeing bondage in Missouri waded across the river into the Quindaro settlement, into freedom, nearly 170 years ago.

An unlikely though distinctly American group of multiracial people founded the settlement – white Massachusetts abolitionists, Black freedmen and freedwomen, and Indigenous people established this town, named literally, "a bundle of sticks," but figuratively, "strength in unity." It remains today as one of the most diverse areas of Kansas. The town, which became a neighborhood and home to America's western-most historically Black university, once embodied our state's identity.

Quindaro helped birth Kansas as well as the noble narrative of the "Free State." Enslaved people fleeing brutal bondage in Missouri and the rest of the Confederate South followed the western Underground Railroad, which passed through Quindaro, cutting a winding path through northeastern Kansas. The town, organized five years before Kansas statehood, mushroomed into a busy frontier outpost.

Quindaro represents our greatest aspirations as a state but also the fragility of our democracy. Democracy must work for everyone or it is not a democracy, and the town began as what the nation at least imagined it could be – a multiracial democracy. It was founded as a haven for enslaved people escaping bondage. "It was one of the first gatherings of people in what we now know as Kansas," said Dr. Shawn Leigh Alexander, the chair of the African and African American Studies Department at the University of Kansas. "We need to understand that it was a multiracial, multi-ethnic burgeoning of a people."

There may not be a better example of a multi-racial democracy anywhere, Alexander said.

But this story isn't about Quindaro the place as much as it is about Quindaro the **idea**. Quindaro, the **vision**. Quindaro, the **aspiration**. Our study of the year 1619 isn't necessarily about Jamestown, Virginia, or about the first Africans to move down the gangplank into lifetimes of brutal servitude. It provides a frame for understanding America, as Quindaro does for Kansas. We can understand not only who we are through this prism, but also who we are supposed to be.

But dark forces beset and besieged Quindaro from the beginning. Riverboat captains encouraged passengers to bypass the town, and slave catchers lurked along the river's edges hunting human property. Others blocked the river, preventing the arrival of supplies in an attempt to smother the town in its infancy.

In the 20th century, as a part of Kansas City, Kansas, segregation made the residents of Quindaro easy targets of police harassment and victims of low property values. Many people fled the area because of that. Then the federal government drove Interstate 635 right through its heart, a near-death blow. Roughly twenty years later, it narrowly escaped an attempt to turn it into a landfill, a literal dump.

As recently as the spring of 2022, legislators intent on strangling Black voting power, redrew voting district maps and the state Supreme Court did virtually nothing to protect Black voters in the newly drawn areas.

Today, Quindaro remains largely undeveloped. There's virtually no investment. The high levels of poverty, if mapped out, align perfectly with bank redlining maps from previous eras.

The arc of this local history embodies the systemic racism ailing Kansas and the nation yet today. In the same way that Kansas serves as America's social fault line (from the Civil War to Prohibition to the Civil Rights Movement to the Summer of Mercy abortion protests), Quindaro's rise and fall reflects the people's aspirations and where the government undermined them.

1820-1850:

As the young United States grew state by state, each new addition to the union was another point of contention that could upset the ever-precarious balance between free and slave states, the see-sawing divide between North and South. It was clear to Congress that, when the Missouri Territory applied for statehood in 1818, a preponderance of the people there would vote to allow slavery. Proponents wanted the state to become the first slave state west of the Mississippi River.

As tensions rose, Congress made numerous attempts to avoid an encroaching war between pro- and anti-slavery states. One of those was the Missouri Compromise of 1820, which admitted Missouri to the Union as a slave state, but also admitted Maine as a free state. As part of the agreement, no territory above the 36-30 line was to enter the Union as a slave state in the future.

Pro-slavery forces still wanted to expand slavery, not only out west in California, where gold had been discovered, but into the Plains, the Rocky Mountains, and the Great Northwest. Anti-slavery forces in the north fought to stop this expansion, resulting in several laws called the Compromise of 1850. California would enter the union as a free state but a vote of the residents —"popular sovereignty" — would determine whether slavery would be allowed in other states formed from the territory the U.S. took from Mexico in 1848.

The 1850 Compromise also abolished the domestic slave trade in the District of Columbia.

Slavers feared Congress — not the states — would pass laws concerning slavery, and abolitionists feared the compromise could lead to an expansion of slavery in new territories.

The Fugitive Slave Act of 1850

A "new" Fugitive Slave Act, also part of the Compromise of 1850, replaced the fugitive slave law that was written into the Constitution, Article 4, Section 2. That provision had been strengthened in the 1793 Fugitive Slave Act. Anyone escaping slavery across state lines must be returned to their owner.

But the third Fugitive Slave Act (1850) required federal marshals to capture and return enslaved people to Southern enslavers and paid them twice as much for deciding a person would be sent South into slavery — $10 for a person sent South and $5 for a runaway set free. Northerners were especially angered by the provision that anyone who assisted someone in escaping from slavery would be fined $1,000 for each person assisted and sent to jail for six months.

Northerners now found intolerable this federal government encroachment on states' rights.

The law forced people who disagreed with or even abhorred slavery to participate in the furtherance of the "peculiar institution," even though many states in the North enacted new personal-liberty laws that stated the federal government could not supersede the state. The number of abolitionists increased, coinciding with a more efficiently implemented Underground Railroad.

The Kansas-Nebraska Act of 1854

The Missouri Compromise held the nation together for thirty-four years before the Kansas-Nebraska Act of 1854 rescinded it.

U.S. Senator Stephen Douglas, an Illinois Democrat, introduced a measure to organize Kansas Territory and the Nebraska Territory, a sprawling and geographically diverse area that included what is now Montana and the Dakotas. New states formed here would vote on whether to allow slavery. This made it possible for slavery to expand into those areas where it had been banned by the Missouri Compromise.

Douglas needed Southern votes to pass his bill, so he attached an amendment that rescinded the Missouri Compromise and created the states of Kansas and Nebraska. Settlers in each, under the principle of popular sovereignty, would vote on whether to permit slavery.

The showdown was at hand.

Pro-slavery settlers poured into Kansas attempting to drag it into slavery while so-called Free Soilers fought those efforts. The battle grew gruesome and bloody, earning our state the moniker Bleeding Kansas.

The Whig Party collapsed under the weight of the debate over this law, and the Democratic party split roughly between the North and South. During a particularly heated debate, Rep. Preston Brooks of South Carolina beat anti-slavery firebrand Sen. Charles Sumner of Massachusetts with a cane on the floor of the Senate.

The Republican Party formed in opposition to the Act and became the nation's leading anti-slavery political party.

As tensions rose, abolitionists needed a new, western route for the Underground Railroad to help people escape bondage in Missouri. Hence they established a town on the Kansas bank of the Missouri River.

Quindaro (Gerald Norwood Collection, Wichita)

A Boom Town and Exodusters

Quindaro, the township, blossomed, standing as a lighthouse for the tempest-tossed enslaved people across the river. Freedom and the idea of a multiracial democracy formed the town's foundation.

According to the Kansas Historical Society, Wyandot Indians had initially purchased that plot of land but when the tribe disbanded, tribal members who wanted to become U.S. citizens divided it among themselves. Among those was Abelard Guthrie and his wife, Nancy Quindaro Brown Guthrie, for whom the town was named.

Wyandots were sympathetic to abolitionism and were active in the Underground Railroad in their native Ohio. The U.S. government forced them to move west "on the heels of the Trail of Tears."

Abelard Guthrie had been adopted into the tribe after he married Nancy and served as vice president of the Quindaro Township Co. He advocated fervently for the town. At its height, its population soared to more than 1,000 according to historical sources.

The town featured homes and several businesses, including the territory's largest sawmill. Quindaro's "lower townsite," near the river, formed its commercial center. Most homes stood higher on a bluff.

One hundred buildings were completed in the town's first year, "including hotels, dry goods, hardware and grocery stores," as well as two churches and a schoolhouse.

The town offered a safe landing for free state settlers as well as those fleeing slavery's terrors. Charles Robinson, who eventually became the first governor of Kansas, wanted to pave the way for settlers to get to the territory.

Robinson, along with Abelard Guthrie, urged the purchase of the land that became Quindaro, and Nancy proved instrumental in convincing her tribe to sell.

The town flourished because it was the best known destination for free soil settlers bound for the Kansas territory. According to Robinson, "The whole free-state world seemed bound for Quindaro."

A drooping national economy and the township's inability to secure a rail line, however, damaged the fledgling town's fortunes, particularly as many of the young men there left in 1861 to join the Union forces in the Civil War.

Some of Quindaro's early residents became members of the First Kansas Colored Regiment of the Civil War.

After the war, freedmen and freedwomen moved to Quindaro. As the population grew, residents established Freedman's University (later chartered as Western University) on the bluff where the old township had once stood. Douglass Hospital would follow.

The first classes at Freedman's University took place in 1862 in the home of Eben Blachley, who taught the children of freedmen and freedwomen.

According to family legend, the white Presbyterian minister from Wisconsin was once nearly hanged as a spy by the Confederate Army. He'd ventured into harm's way looking for his son, who'd been captured by the Confederates.

But with a noose around his neck, the Confederates allowed him some last words, and after praying out loud for the Confederates' souls because they were about to hang an innocent man, they "took the noose off his neck and sent him home to Wisconsin."

That experience reportedly caused Eben Blachley to dedicate his life to helping the formerly enslaved at the school.

In 1872, the state increased the school's funding to establish a four-year program to train teachers and by the 1880s, the mass movement of African Americans leaving the South for Kansas boosted the population in the state and at the school. That movement was called the Exoduster Movement and participants, Exodusters.

Also about that time, the African Methodist Episcopal Conference began providing financial support to the school, which added a theological course and built Ward Hall to accommodate it.

By 1911, students, faculty and churches raised $2,000 to erect a statue of abolitionist John Brown. That statue is the last vestige of the school, the community, or the town still standing.

The second institution of note in Quindaro, Douglass Hospital, was the first Black community-owned hospital west of the Mississippi to treat any and all patients regardless of their race, according to Deborah Dandridge, associate librarian at the Kenneth Spencer Research Library at the University of Kansas.

Until the 1960s, Black doctors and nurses in the U.S. were denied access to most hospitals, and most Black patients were either not accepted at all or relegated to inferior, segregated areas in hospitals, such as hallways and basements. (Even today, access to quality health care remains out of reach to many African Americans.)

Again, Quindaro proved ahead of its time.

Dandridge said Black doctors and community leaders organized the hospital, named for the renowned abolitionist and journalist Frederick Douglass, in December 1898. It provided 10 patient beds on its first floor, and nurses' quarters on the second floor.

Patient admissions plummeted in the 1930s. The school had graduated 43 nurses during the previous three decades, but the Douglass Hospital Training School closed in 1937.

In 1945, with the support of the greater Kansas City community and federal funding, Douglass renovated a three story building on the former Western University campus to accommodate a 50-bed hospital that included a blood bank, lab and an obstetrics unit.

By 1954 however, desegregation practices in area hospitals were eroding admissions, eventually leading to Douglass' closure in 1977. The building was then torn down and its records lost, Dandridge said.

But integration giveth and also taketh away. As the old saying goes, people got the integration they wanted, but in the process, lost the community cohesion and independent businesses they once had. In explicit and implicit ways, integration disintegrated Black communities.

Prolonged Troubles

With its proud history and its university and hospital, Quindaro had at first experienced a kind of golden age. It became a community beloved by the people who lived and worshipped there. Its progeny remain fiercely loyal and deeply proud of Quindaro and its heritage.

But upstream opponents gathered to prevent Quindaro from receiving supplies and patrolled the river banks to claw freedmen and freedwomen back into bondage.

Segregation —which spread across the nation from the 1870s to the 1920s and remained until the mid-to-late 1960s— kept Quindaro socially and economically isolated. Black residents in neighborhoods like Quindaro found it difficult or even dangerous to venture too far beyond the town.

Police reinforced those societal norms, and the Kansas City metro area's economy conveniently left Quindaro and other segregated Black areas behind, more by design than by accident. Some fled the community and, as an unintended consequence, left it weakened.

In the 1960s, Interstate 635 was built, completed in 1975; state and federal governments rammed it through its heart of Quindaro.

As was the case in many cities, including Wichita, St. Louis, and many others, planners devastated Black communities under the guise of "urban renewal" and wiping out blight. Residents in those areas grew to derisively refer to these efforts as "negro removal."

According to current residents, Quindaro was never the same.

In the mid-1980s, a landfill was proposed for the site. It seemed a particularly odd place for a landfill, what with the historical significance and the natural beauty of the tall bluffs overlooking the river.

Nevertheless, the plan moved ahead until it collided with an obscure law.

Under the Kansas Antiquities Commission Act, and because Kansas City owned part of the landfill site and held permitting authority, an investigation of the site had to be conducted.

Over a two-year period, archeologists discovered a cistern, three wells, and the foundations of 22 residential and commercial buildings. That, and a public outcry, caused the landfill company to abandon the project.

What remains is commonly referred to as "the ruins."

When the company pulled out, no funding was provided for the analysis or storage of the nearly 200 cubic feet of excavated artifacts. An agreement passed ownership of the collection to the Kansas Historical Society, which now uses the items for exhibitions and archeological education.

Quindaro escaped an ignominious fate, but that has not deterred the illegal dumping that still goes on there. It remains isolated socially and economically while still clinging to life.

As a neighborhood, it benefits from a deeply loyal base of residents, former residents and Quindaro offspring who still believe that for all the abuse it's endured, it could still achieve the beautiful restored future it deserves as the multiracial democracy it promised seventy years ago. Quindaro is a testament to the durability of a core idea. [A longer piece on Quindaro was published by the ACLU of Kansas.]

5/ Should Black Greeks Rename Their Organizations?

February 20, 2025

In a speech at the University of Minnesota in 2002, the late Randall Robinson, best known for his anti-Apartheid and reparations advocacy, said the following: "Herodotus, the Greek historian, wrote 500 years before Christ that everything Ancient Greece was: its calendar, its division of the year into 12 parts, its language, its math, its science, its gods, its mythology, its carving figures in stone, all of it … had been derived from older civilizations to the south, the civilizations of Egypt and Ethiopia."

Years before I found that speech, I met Asa Hilliard, an educational psychologist and Egyptologist, when he spoke at my church in Louisville, Kentucky. In 1976, Hilliard wrote the introduction for a much-maligned book originally published in 1954 titled *Stolen Legacy.* The book argued that Greek Philosophy was stolen African philosophy.

Given this, and years of reading on these subjects, I've long wondered why Black fraternities and sororities, recently highlighted via the presidential campaign of Vice President Kamala Harris, a member of Alpha Kappa Alpha, haven't dropped Greek letters from their names. Maybe the time has come for this discussion.

I'm not attacking Black Greek organizations. Just the opposite. Some of the most consequential people in my life belong to these organizations.

My brother is a member of Kappa Alpha Psi. My late journalism professor Samuel Adams, a trailblazing Black journalist and someone I called "Daddy Sam," was a member of Omega Psi Phi. Betty Bayé, my colleague at the *Louisville Courier-Journal,* whom I still call "Queen" and greet with a peck on her cheek, is a member of Delta Sigma Theta.

Bayé shared that while her sorority and the other "Divine Nine" have Greek letters in their name, the practice is like everything Black people have done in our sojourn here in the West — we reshaped it and made it our own. We changed the culture.

"Some ate high on the hog and gave us the scraps," she said. "We took the leavings and created 'Soul Food.' The white folks gave us their version of the Bible to create docile slaves. What did we do? We gave birth to Nat Turner and Black Liberation Theology. We went into newsrooms as suspects unworthy of our jobs. What did we do? We created NABJ to encourage and honor our own."

NABJ is the National Association of Black Journalists.

Mentor Charles F. McAfee, the famed Kansas architect and a member of Kappa Alpha Psi, sponsored my entrance into Sigma Pi Phi, a professional fraternity also known as the "Boule," after college. I didn't follow a traditional path into Black fraternity life (I've been inactive for years), but I have some standing in this discussion.

Black Greek Letter Organizations' emergence, according to the National Museum of African American History and Culture, coincided with "the rise of Jim Crow laws, the popularity of scientific racism, and widespread racial violence."

Today, the nine BGLOs comprise the National Panhellenic Council. Nationwide, these organizations have created community, mentored young professionals and raised scholarship money. These networks lift up entire communities.

But I've felt an incongruity with the organizations maintaining connection to the Greeks, who we know traveled to Africa to study.

As the 1990s hip-hop group, The X-Clan, said: "I am an African, I don't wear Greek. Must I be reminded of a legendary thief who tried to make Greece in comparison to Egypt?"

This isn't disparagement. I'm invoking a common paradox for African Americans: managing the "twoness" that W.E.B. DuBois described of people trying to inhabit a larger, hostile society while retaining a sense of self.

I'd experienced this sort of cultural awakening as a young adult.

I'd read the *Autobiography of Malcolm X* before my junior year in college. In my dorm room, I played my mother's old Dr. Martin Luther King Jr. records on a loop. Researching a term paper for my History of American Journalism class, in which we each wrote about the year of our birth, I discovered the Black Panthers and the fire-breathing H. Rap Brown.

My campus friends and I brought Malcolm X's widow Betty Shabazz and educator Jawanza Kunjufu to campus. We travelled to Kansas City Kansas to hear Yousef Ben-Jochannan, known as "Dr. Ben." I earned a journalism degree with an African and African American Studies emphasis.

In Louisville, where I landed my first post-college job, I joined St. Stephen Baptist Church, still led by the Rev. Kevin W. Cosby, who guided me toward more knowledge.

St. Stephen offered an Afrocentric lifestyles ministry, where we could adopt African names. But for my father's pride in our family history, I would have taken the surname "Makalani," which among varied definitions means "writer." We had a "Rites of Passage" program for youth that I helped lead. We named our Family Life Center after activist Fanny Lou Hamer. We flew a red, black and green flag out front.

But meeting Hilliard there left an indelible mark on Mark.

Hilliard introduced me to historian John Henrick Clarke's work. Clarke once famously said it was "impossible to continue to oppress a consciously historical people." My fraternity brother named his son Asa after Hilliard.

Some Black people reject the term African American. They've argued they've never been to Africa and know nothing of it. They consider themselves American, not African. Still, African Americans have increasingly embraced their African heritage. It is no longer unusual to see Jesus depicted as Black in Black churches. More Black people now wear their hair naturally or braided. They wear Ankhs and Kente cloth.

Amid this reawakening, maybe it's time to discuss this name change.

A *Stolen Legacy* review included this passage: "The greatest crime Europe committed against the world was the intellectual theft of Africa's heritage. Empires were stolen, whole countries snatched and named after pirates, rapists, and swindlers. Palaces and monumental edifices destroyed could be rebuilt, but when you steal a people's cultural patrimony and use it to enslave, colonize and insult them, then you've committed unforgivable acts bordering on sacrilege."

Enslavers tortured our names, language, and culture out of us. Few of us can trace our lineage beyond the slave trade. A name change for Black Greek organizations could help with cultural reformation.

I recently ran across a 1963 radio interview with Malcolm X where the interviewer asked about his "X." Malcolm explained that enslavers ripped away their captives' names, replacing them with a slave master's surname connoting ownership. "X" signifies the unknown in mathematics, so he replaced his slave name with "X."

Malcolm said if you saw a Japanese or Chinese person named Barney Murphy (I inserted a first name), it likely would confuse some folks. The same holds true for African Americans with names like Murphy or O'Kelly or McCormick. These names don't reflect our African origins. They typically reflect the horrors we've endured. The humiliations we suffered. The swaths of history torn away.

Why should we wear such names?

Exactly.

6/ Kansas' Shared History with Apartheid South Africa

May 28, 2025

Former U.S. Senator Nancy Kassebaum served as chairwoman of the Senate Subcommittee on African Affairs and helped develop sanctions against the apartheid regime of South Africa. (Thad Allton for Kansas Reflector)

During my 1980s college years, our student group urged the university to divest from any South African interests. Many campuses nationwide saw students protesting that country's legalized system of racial oppression, apartheid.

In that era, roughly 30 years from the civil rights movement, the fight against apartheid had gained traction in politics and in popular culture. The 1985 protest song "Sun City" played on a loop on video music shows, while President Reagan seemingly coddled the regime.

Most people, however, may have forgotten the role of Kansas and the United States in this winding human rights saga.

First, some perspective. Today white South Africans represent 7 percent of the population but own 72 percent of the land. Black South Africans represent 81 percent of the population but own 4 percent of the land.

White South Africans are not oppressed, though the late comedian Robin Williams once rhetorically asked the white minority there: "Does the name Custer mean anything to you?"

Apartheid, which means "apartness," mirrored American racial segregation. A person's race determined where people could live, where they could work, and whom they could marry.

This month, President Trump ambushed South African President Cyril Ramaphosa during a White House meeting, peddling a false narrative of "white genocide" there. Trump, while aggressively deporting immigrants of color, recently welcomed 59 white South Africans who he claimed were fleeing oppression. If there is a genocide, why are only 59 people trying to escape it?

It's important to note that truth matters little to this president. What is important is the continued building of a false, white grievance narrative for his base. He's reassuring them that he's for them. Always.

The more news media press him about this, the deeper and wider his base's roots of loyalty strengthen and spread.

Nevertheless, Kansas and America had an interesting connection with South Africa, apartheid, and with the jailing and eventual release of Nelson

Mandela, who would eventually rule the nation that imprisoned him.

Former U.S. Sen. Nancy Kassebaum, then chairwoman of the Senate Subcommittee on African Affairs, helped develop sanctions against the apartheid regime.

President Reagan vetoed the legislation, but Congress overrode his veto. The sanctions, along with international pressure, helped dismantle that system.

A Kansan stood watch over apartheid on its deathbed.

President Clinton dispatched Ronald Walters, the noted political science expert and co-architect of the historic Dockum sit-in, to South Africa to monitor elections that would spell the end of apartheid.

Walters, also an architect of the Congressional Black Caucus, knew Mandela, who phoned the Walters' home in 2010 after Walters died.

Another Kansan, Gretchen Eick, now a retired professor of history and award-winning author, lobbied against apartheid for 30 years and was part of the final 1986 passage of comprehensive sanctions over Reagan's veto.

"A stunning experience!" Eick wrote via email.

Kansas Attorney General Kris Kobach, who researched apartheid as a Harvard student in the 1980s, told *The Wichita Eagle* years ago that he'd grown interested in South Africa because its issues had reached that campus. Kobach said then that he didn't oppose sanctions, but he thought disinvestment removed American companies from the fight. Those companies, he said, could form a powerful anti-apartheid bloc.

He reportedly wrote his senior thesis at Harvard about how South African businesses had become politicized. Kobach based that report, for which he won a campus award, on research conducted during a 1987 visit to South Africa.

Harvard professor Samuel Huntington advised Kobach's work, and reportedly believed South Africa should pursue a "policy of simultaneous reform and repression," said a review in *The Harvard Crimson*, the student newspaper.

Black South Africans faced brutal repression, and the U.S., under President Kennedy, helped imprison Mandela.

NPR, in a 2016 interview with a former CIA official, reported Mandela's 1962 capture happened because of a U.S. tip to South African officials. That capture and arrest led to Mandela's nearly 28-year imprisonment.

According to *Time* magazine, when the South African government released Mandela in 1990, the *Atlanta Journal-Constitution* quoted a "senior CIA operative" regarding Mandela's capture.

Within hours of Mandela's arrest, operative Paul Eckel said: "We have turned Mandela over to the South African security branch. We gave them every detail, what he would be wearing, the time of day, just where he would be. They have picked him up. It is one of our greatest coups."

Our country played dual roles in Mandela's life.

It delivered him to his captors but also lobbied South Africa not to hang him for treason and later applied political and economic pressure to end apartheid.

And our "Free State," played a small role in Mandela's and in that nation's liberation.

7/ Oklahoma Tour Shows Freedom Is a Perpetual Climb

June 22, 2025

While touring Pawhuska, Oklahoma, columnist Mark McCormick captured this image of several sets of stairs, ascending upward and upward. (Mark McCormick for Kansas Reflector)

The Greenwood Rising Center in Tulsa features a James Baldwin quote on its exterior: "Not everything that is faced can be changed, but nothing can be changed until it is faced."

It's built atop the site where one of the nation's greatest Black surgeons had hunkered down during terrifying nights of violence, only to walk outside the following morning, his gifted hands raised, to be gunned down by a mob.

During a recent tour in Oklahoma, with members of the Church of the Resurrection, we saw monuments and markers of two of the deadliest acts of racial violence in American history — Tulsa's Greenwood and the Osage murders.

Despite Baldwin's quote, nothing's really being faced on that corner. Not in nearby Pawhuska, where the Osage murders unfolded. Not in a country where neo-Nazis and white supremacists continue marching with renewed vigor.

We remain in a perpetual approach pattern, where we descend but never land on justice. We measure racial progress in America by the pace of white acknowledgment, and during current Juneteenth celebrations, we should remember that freedom isn't a destination.

It remains an endless climb.

A couple of weeks ago however, Tulsa's Greenwood district and Pawhuska marked destinations for the Adult Discipleship Ministry billed by the group's leader and my dear friend, the Rev. Robert Johnson, as definitely "not a vacation."

This "human rights immersion" trip, inspired by church Senior Pastor Adam Hamilton, sold out online in 43 minutes, which spoke to the earnest desires of the group to learn how discipleship must have social as well as personal expressions.

"You will be expected to engage in intense learning and discipleship-building exercises," Johnson's preparatory missive to the group read.

Johnson's charming wife, Linda, kept us on pace for all our stops.

We saw monument after monument in Tulsa.

We saw a statue of the iconic historian John Hope Franklin, the son of a prominent Greenwood lawyer who had written real-time notes of black, fiery, turpentine balls dropping from planes strafing the 36-BLOCK, the Black business district.

We gathered around solemn black monuments in front of the Greenwood Cultural Center that offered a register of Black businesses destroyed. We paused over rectangular plaques embedded in the sidewalks in front of the only remaining buildings from old Greenwood.

We saw murals and remembrances under the Interstate 244 bridge that state and local officials drove through the heart of Greenwood, intent on strangling the vaunted business district. We saw the refurbished Mt. Vernon Baptist Church, burned in the massacre.

Our Greenwood tour guide, Kode Ransom, explained deftly what rarely garners mention in the massacre's lore. There was no record made identifying a single white looter or white victim of rape.

Ransom said that by 1933, Greenwood had rebuilt itself, only to have construction of I-244 and urban renewal destroy much of what had been rebuilt.

Members of the Church of the Resurrection visited monuments and markers of two of the deadliest acts of racial violence in American history. (Mark McCormick for Kansas Reflector)

After a day and an evening in Greenwood, we moved an hour northeast to Pawhuska, the site of the Osage murders resurrected by David Gann's book and the Martin Scorsese film, *Killers of the Flower Moon.*

The book and film detail the theft of wildly profitable oil rights from Osage people. The Osage selected the rocky, barren land as a barrier to white interest, but those hopes died, as did many Osage, when oil was discovered there.

Historians often teach the Greenwood massacre and the Osage murders in tandem since they occurred in roughly the same area, in the same era, each with white greed and envy fueling orgies of violence.

Outside the Osage Nation Museum, we saw still more monuments.

We saw a granite memorial for the Osage veterans with a giant feather in the center. Another monument rose from the ground like a huge headstone with etchings saying the petroleum industry had gifted the slab.

Another nearby featured a seated, majestic Chief Claremore, weapons in each hand.

The monuments — from Greenwood to Pawhuska — harkened Carl Hines Jr.'s words: "Dead men make such convenient heroes for they cannot rise to challenge the images we would fashion from their lives and besides, it is easier to build monuments than to build a better world."

Bodies likely remain under a new baseball field in Greenwood. Many more bodies have not been discovered. Killers dumped still more in the cloudy brown Arkansas River.

Society's response?

You can have all the museums and monuments you want, just don't ask for justice. This process of misremembering and denial is designed to preserve the innocence of one group, at the expense of another.

It's a pattern visible since the Confederacy's "Lost Cause" narrative after the Civil War. Look closely, and there's a bloody thread running from the Appomattox Courthouse to Greenwood, to a dozen other massacres, to George Floyd, to Jan. 6, 2021.

Deny the obvious and blame the victims.

We hear this denial in the following familiar assertions: "The Civil War wasn't about slavery." "The slaves were happy." The Civil War was the "war of northern aggression." "Black men (trying to prevent the lynching of a falsely accused man) started the Greenwood Massacre." "George Floyd was a drug addict." "Jan. 6 was a day of love."

Attempt to erase evidence. Rip out newspaper accounts. Ban it from being taught in schools. Remove the evidence from museums, archives, and government websites. Pardon participants. Never speak of what happened. When that doesn't work, willfully misremember it.

When none of that works, argue that rehashing the past is pointless. Eventually, while denying any culpability or remuneration, grudgingly grant the smallest modicum of acknowledgment: a monument. Then relax while grief and terror get monetized.

Wash, rinse, repeat.

This has remained true even of Juneteenth, the supposed date when Texas' enslaved people learned about their freedom. Enslaved people knew already. It was the people who "owned" people who were learning they could no longer keep people hostage.

This is the cycle Pastor Adam, the Rev. Robert and Linda wanted to shatter with the human rights tour. On the trip back, I offered another James Baldwin quotation: "To act is to be committed, and to be committed is to be in danger."

So no, freedom can't be a destination.

It's a perpetual climb.

8/ Kansas No Kings Rally: A Call to Remember our Past

October 28, 2025

A variety of causes pulled people into the joyful throngs of the Oct. 18 No Kings demonstrations, despite masked federal agents ramming cars and snatching racially ambiguous people from American streets.

Joyous because songs, smiles and hugs, and inflatable costumes filled the atmosphere and pierced the loneliness and fear that escalating immigration raids and National Guard occupation threats have created. At the rallies, immigration advocates risked their safety to encourage those living in the shadows. LGBTQ+ advocates asserted their intention to live unapologetically. Organizers sounded a civic engagement call to action.

Cheers affirmed each perspective, a contrast to belched accusations from event detractors who claimed that participants hate America.

But my concern as a speaker at the Overland Park rally centered on an already dismantled cause, one worth fighting to restore.

I referenced a recent morning news appearance by Wright Thompson, the noted author of *The Barn: The Secret History of a Murder in Mississippi*. He said his readers believe that those in charge of government want a return to a pre-Civil Rights America.

It seems that way.

Former MSNBC anchor Joy Reid said the MAGA movement now "has everything it wanted."

She said MAGA has control of the White House, both chambers of Congress and an obedient Supreme Court that has imbued the executive branch with seemingly unlimited power. The court, she said, has allowed racial profiling. Masked ICE agents can stop Latino people based on their appearance and accents. MAGA has ended diversity, equity, and inclusion. It has ended affirmative action.

"You get all the best jobs even if you're not qualified," she said, referencing Pete Hegseth moving from Fox weekend news anchor to the head of the Department of War (Defense) and Kash Patel moving from podcasting to running the FBI.

MAGA has banned books, banned *The 1619 Project*, smothered Black history in museums and dared historians to tell the truth.

"You've canceled Black scholarships. You're damned near getting rid of HBCs (Historically Black Colleges and Universities). The president has already said they're not going to serve minority-serving institutions," she said. "What more do you want? You said you wanted your country back. Now, you've got it."

It feels as though half the nation has backtracked on once foundational ideas such as freedom of and *from* religion, separation of church and state, and a common good.

While this movement unfolds, the rest of us wonder how we're going to live with people who spend every waking moment thinking of new ways to manage our lives. A dear friend said that because of these differences, he envisioned a future America organized like the European Union, with states or regions operating as nation states. We'd share economies and defense structures but live separately.

You can reasonably argue that we've never actually been "e pluribus unum," out of many, one. Not with slavery, not with the destruction of Indigenous people, not with limited rights for women, not with inequality that always has existed.

The No Kings participants don't hate America. They hate how people can't understand unfairness until it happens to them. They hate hollow religiosity. They hate how half the nation keeps reviving our racial caste system.

This tracks with my closing message.

Thompson told his interviewers that while standing on the bank of the Tallahatchie River in Mississippi with one of Emmett Till's relatives and staring into the water, the relative said, "I'm just so grateful."

"Grateful?" He didn't understand.

"Because he got out of the river," she replied, and it clicked for Thompson.

He said the Tallahatchie is known as the "singing river" for all the lynched bodies tossed into it, bodies that yet today cry out for justice.

That's important, Thompson said, because so many people in the country today want to put Emmett and all such history back into the Tallahatchie. To drown it. To forget it. Symbolically then, we must get out of the water, onto the banks and into a movement to ensure immigration advocates don't have to risk their safety, where our LGBTQ+ loved ones can live freely, where civic engagement is our default.

So many of us are just trying to keep our heads above water, but we must drag ourselves and as many others as we can out of the river and into a movement that protects what we have and restores what we've lost.

We have to get out of that river, before our Democracy sinks to the bottom.

9/ 1965 Wichita Plane Crash Left Families Locked in a Moment

January 10, 2023

After a fully fueled KC-135 military tanker crashed into what was then a segregated Wichita neighborhood, my sister Chan chose not to believe our 5-year-old cousin, Tracy Randolph, had died in the fiery 1965 disaster.

Chandra McCormick, weeks from her 12th birthday, watched soap operas with our great-grandmother, Jessie Pearl Holloway, whom we called Big Mama. Chan borrowed a common storyline from the shows and told herself Tracy had just lost her memory. When her amnesia lifted, Tracy would come home.

But that Saturday morning crash — still considered Kansas' deadliest air disaster — killed 30 people, including Tracy, our grandmother Mary Daniels (we called her Little Mama), our uncle C.L. Daniels and our cousin Clyde Holloway.

Documentarians Kevin Harrison, Riccardo Harris and Kenneth Hawkins want to re-examine the grief of survivors from that Jan. 16 morning — people either carrying that grief and continuing to live, or those who coped by existing because living felt impossible.

Interviewing them convinced me that I needed to look no further than my childhood household for various expressions of grief, though my mother and my aunt almost never spoke of it.

The tanker had just left McConnell Air Force Base outside Wichita but struggled to climb. As a crash seemed imminent, the crew began dumping fuel, but the plane dived into a vacant lot. A cascade of 32,000 gallons of jet fuel and fire incinerated a dozen homes.

The entire crew died. The crash gouged a crater 15 feet deep. The emotional trauma ran deeper. Several children died, as did an entire family. The accident left others homeless.

A Kansas Historical Society article praised the initial disaster response but said "that help started to wane." It described the temporary survivor housing as "rundown and unsafe."

It described the legal settlements as "disappointing."

"One family received just $400," the article said, while the average settlement stood at $13,000, minus the 20% that went to attorney fees. Many survivors wondered whether the payouts would have been more substantial had they been white.

Segregation, according to D.W. Carter, author of *Mayday Over Wichita*, forced Black people into a small area, boosting the death toll. Wichita then ranked as one of the nation's most segregated cities.

The documentary intends to excavate all this ground.

"My interest in this story increased as I learned more about the victims," said Harris, who is my cousin and executive director of GEAR UP at Wichita State University. I attended KU with both him and Harrison in the late 1980s. "I hope the unheard voices of the victims — those who died and those left behind — can finally be heard and understood."

Harrison, an assistant professor for the Cohen Honor College at WSU, said previous books and films about the crash didn't sufficiently examine survivors' emotions.

"Every rung of <u>Maslow's ladder</u> expresses the desire to be heard and understood," Harrison said, referring to the model of basic human needs. "This project was an opportunity to give a voice to the voiceless."

Harrison said previous projects identified victims' names and addresses. He intends to dig deeper.

"Stories give us power," he said. "I want to explore real emotion."

A $10,000 Kansas Humanities Council grant funds the project, along with a partnership with Omega Psi Phi Fraternity. Robert Weems Jr., a professor of Business History at WSU serves as project consultant. They plan to screen the film at the park near the crash site this spring.

I wasn't born until 1967. Still, the crash never seemed far away.

I was an adult, for example, before learning from my sister that my aunt Laura Faust, Tracy's mother, doted over every boy-child in the family, but never had much to do with the girls, who likely reminded her too much of Tracy. Much of what I know, my sister shared.

Chan shared a particularly cruel story about witnesses claiming to have seen a child, engulfed in flames, running from one of the homes and collapsing. Someone asked our aunt if that child was Tracy.

Horrified, I asked how she replied.

"She didn't," Chan said. "She just closed her eyes and lowered her head."

When loved ones die, "what ifs" and our memories can act as comforting counterweights when pain starts to circle. But with a child, the what ifs must seem gargantuan because of what the child never had a chance to become. My aunt suffered quietly, dying at 65.

My sister planned to visit our grandmother's house that morning but overslept.

She awoke to my aunt leaving to drop Tracy at Little Mama's. Chan started walking there later, but along the way, the ground shook and black smoke filled the air. Where our grandmother's house stood, she saw a lake of fire.

"I was numb," she said. "It didn't seem real."

The grief stricken can find themselves locked in a moment, compressing a traumatizing incident into perhaps its worst instant.

A child might do what my sister did, create a magical narrative as a means of coping.

An adult might do what my aunt Laura did — hold it in, withdraw, and struggle through life existing because she couldn't peel back enough of the grief to really live.

People grieve differently, doing their best to move from one moment to the next and secure some semblance of safety and control.

In 1965's segregated Wichita, neither our family nor our neighbors — however we grieved — really had much of either.

10/ Learning from Tulsa's Reckoning with Greenwood

August 18, 2023 published in *The Journal:
A Civic Issues Magazine*

In confronting the 1921 race massacre that left the Greenwood neighborhood in ruins, Tulsa is attempting to manage factions, expectations and progress. But the going gets tough when accounting for losses incurred in the past means accountability for those in the present.

Novelist Charles Dickens wrote *A Tale of Two Cities,* but had he traveled to Tulsa, he'd have found at least four.

Segregation created Greenwood, a separate town where in the early 20th century one group flourished despite boundaries designed to suffocate its aspirations. In fact, the segregated group did too well. Climbed too high. Accomplished too much. So much, that segregationists descended violently on that part of Tulsa, burning and looting and killing hundreds of people and then marching survivors into holding camps to "maintain order."

A heavy curtain of silence then fell over the community, which quickly got busy forgetting and misremembering. Few spoke about the horrors of May 31 through June 1, 1921. Decades of silence created more cities inside the city. More places where time and the cold pressure of a collective secret further divided residents.

The secret that Tulsa protected for decades is more widely known today, profiled in numerous news reports and podcasts and vividly re-created in the HBO TV series *Watchmen.* A white mob destroyed a nearly 40-square-block Greenwood area of Tulsa, known as Black Wall Street because of the successful businesses there. Members of the Tulsa Police Department, the Tulsa Chamber of Commerce, the Tulsa County Sheriff's Department as well as the Oklahoma National Guard and assorted other municipal leaders made up the mob.

The marauders killed hundreds of Black residents, injured thousands more and burned down more than 1,000 homes and businesses but not before looting those homes and businesses. Damage estimates range as high as $200 million in today's dollars. The number of homeless was put at 9,000.

As the centennial of the race massacre approached, a group of residents began raising money for a commemoration of the event and to announce a plan to make sure the community, the state and, yes, the nation, would not only remember what happened, but learn how to create a more just society where something similar could never happen again.

But as donations mounted, schisms formed between Black factions. One faction believed that since fundraisers used the likenesses and travails of survivors, then surely, some of the $30 million raised should go to those three survivors as reparations. The fundraisers, though, believed the money should fund educational projects and that the government should pay survivors, not the educational fund.

The notion of reparations divided white Tulsans too. The 1921 Tulsa Race Massacre Centennial Commission excused the white mayor as a member after he said reparations would divide the community. The commission also ejected the state's white governor after he pushed through a measure prohibiting the teaching of certain racial topics in Oklahoma classrooms.

Here is where this historic oil town finds itself today, caught under a gusher of history. There are centenarians deserving restitution. Still others, in oil-patch parlance, want this gusher capped and for the history that has surfaced to be shut-in along with all the civic, legal and financial responsibilities flowing from those terrible days. The city is learning how real racial reconciliation can't occur without a reckoning. There's hope here, however, despite the tensions.

The story of Tulsa and the efforts of its people to reckon with its past is a fitting case study for Kansans and the country at large to consider as Americans continue to wrestle with the nation's history and our differing interpretations of that history. It's a tale about the limits of good intentions and how resistance to loss in the present can continue to divide us even as we seek to remedy the losses of the past.

No one's from here

Americans can get pretty Pollyannaish about race. We seem to want reconciliation without the requisite reckoning – a real examination of the systems that produced social inequality. Mere discussions or shallow friendships get mistaken for actual progress. However, real understanding develops in real depth.

That's what Greenwood Rising Executive Director Raymond Doswell believes is happening at his relatively new history center, as well as in the community at large. It is a place with a better shot at reconciliation than most, he says.

"That's the whole thing about Tulsa. It was built by people coming from other places. People looking for their fortune. People looking for a better life."

His organization is trying to create a community out of individuals brought there by the four winds. Every Tulsa Public Schools eighth-grader comes through the history center, and there's even a carve-out allowing for the teaching of this history despite an edict pushed through the Oklahoma Legislature by Gov. Kevin Stitt in the wake of panic over critical race theory. Every police academy recruit comes through, as well as officers from other cities such as Wichita.

It remains one of the few places actually designed for the kinds of conversations the culture must have.

"We're on a journey toward reconciliation," says Doswell, who formerly served as curator at the Negro Leagues Baseball Museum in Kansas City, Missouri. "We want you to talk about it. We encourage dialogue."

Doswell said he's seen strangers strike up conversations at the history center and watched the momentum of those conversations carry the visitors out of the building and on to dinner for more discussion.

What's discussed at the history center, he says, "is an ugly truth about the country."

Doswell points out that as the pandemic began to slow, it did not slow fast enough for some people who were eager and even impatient for a return to normal. There's a similar desire for a kind of racial normalcy. But as was the case with the pandemic, we've been changed by what has happened. We'll never get back to normal. We're going to have to adjust to a new normal.

"I think that's happening," he says.

Doswell declined to address it, but most observers agreed that the pall over the city has to do with reparations.

Archaeologists continue to search for mass grave sites following the discovery of one group of coffins using ground-penetrating radar/sonar.

Tensions remain taut. In 2015, a white reserve sheriff's deputy shot and killed Eric Harris during an arrest. The next year, Officer Betty Shelby fatally shot Terence Crutcher while his hands were raised. In 2020, following the deaths elsewhere of Ahmaud Arbery, Breonna Taylor and George Floyd, demonstrators briefly blocked Interstate 44. That prompted the state's Republican-controlled legislature to pass a law providing legal immunity in some cases to motorists who run down demonstrators on roadways.

Race still divides people here in life – the city remains relatively segregated – and in death, as those excavations found.

Honest differences

James Goodwin's family survived the 1921 Tulsa massacre. One of his relatives, a fair-complexioned Black man, stood on his porch and because he looked white, he was able to wave the mob away.

His family, which owns and publishes the state's oldest Black-owned newspaper, *The Oklahoma Eagle*, stayed in Greenwood and rebuilt their lives. It was an achievement, but Tulsa was not done with Greenwood.

In the 1950s, the state and federal governments drove an interstate highway through the neighborhood — in much the same way other Black communities across the nation were destroyed. The government called it urban renewal. African Americans called it "Negro removal." The highway put the final nail in the coffin of Greenwood's prosperity. Goodwin said there are plans underway to reclaim a wide section of old Greenwood that the highway now covers.

Attorney and *Oklahoma Eagle* publisher James Goodwin sees hope for a new Greenwood if a 30-acre section of the community now covered by a highway can be reclaimed. "We can re-create a Black business community," he says.

Goodwin would like to see seedlings for a new Greenwood sprinkled there where Black Wall Street could be reborn.

"The removal of the highway will free up 30 acres," says Goodwin, who is also a lawyer. "We can re-create a Black business community."

The community received a $1.5 million grant from the federal government in an effort that his niece, State Rep. Regina Goodwin, spearheaded, to eliminate the highway exchange.

Now, two entities in Greenwood, the new Greenwood Rising history center, and the established Greenwood Cultural Center, have formed a fault line. The buildings stand relatively close, but a real distance in focus exists between them.

Goodwin says many Black residents hoped both entities would advance together, but Greenwood Rising has received significantly more support. They also think that because images and stories of the survivors were used to fundraise for Greenwood

Rising, some of that money should go to the centenarian survivors. Other Black residents think segments of the community are just waiting for the survivors to die.

A failed centennial event two years ago, meant to memorialize the tragedy, offered a sense of how deep divisions go between Black factions.

Leaders of the 1921 Tulsa Race Massacre Centennial Commission organized a mammoth Memorial Day weekend event at the community's minor league baseball stadium, featuring award-winning songwriter and performer John Legend, and former Georgia gubernatorial candidate and voting rights advocate Stacey Abrams. The event, Remember and Rise, collapsed days before it was to be held.

A smoldering debate erupted over who should compensate massacre survivors. One group stated that the commission, which had raised $30 million, should compensate survivors. Members of the commission stated that since government actors participated in the attack, government should pay the reparations. They weren't necessarily opposed to reparations, just not from their pool of funds.

Oklahoma State Sen. Kevin Matthews founded and chaired the centennial commission that promoted the holiday event as a way to share Greenwood's story. Matthews and the commission earmarked the money that it raised almost exclusively for a history exhibit, art projects and a cultural center in the neighborhood.

On the other side of the debate stood Damario Solomon-Simmons, a lawyer representing survivors in a lawsuit against the city and a range of city and state entities involved in the marauding and aftermath. It's Solomon-Simmons' position that the commission raised money using images of the massacre but used the money for a building when some of the funds should have gone to survivors and descendants.

To try to rescue the Memorial Day events, the *New York Times* reported that Matthews and the commission negotiated 11th hour, $100,000 direct payments to each survivor as well as $2 million to establish a reparations fund, which the legal team initially accepted – only to return the next day asking for significantly more. Further talks and the planned events then crumbled.

A couple of decades earlier, the state had made a gesture toward reconciliation. In 1997, the legislature established a commission that studied the riot. It recommended that the state pay reparations and build a memorial to the dead. In 2001, the legislature passed the 1921 Race Riot Reconciliation Act. The legislation did not include reparations, nor did it provide funding for any initiatives, despite the commission's conclusion that reparations "would be good public policy and do much to repair the emotional and physical scars of this terrible incident in our shared past."

So much of what has happened in Oklahoma's racial history is in fact difficult to face.

Black Wall Street attacked

The destruction of Greenwood came about largely because Black success was an unspeakable indignity to white supremacists. It tragically represents the kind of inclusive prosperity that politicians and governments often say they want to create in this day and age.

"Imagine a community of great possibilities and prosperity built by Black people for Black people," The *New York Times* wrote. "Places to work. Places to live. Places to learn and shop and play. Places to worship."

In the 100 block of Greenwood Avenue, for instance, more than 70 businesses operated out of red brick buildings, The *Times* reported, with all but a couple owned by Black entrepreneurs. Because segregation excluded Black Tulsans from shopping at many white-owned businesses, Black Wall Street created a self-sufficient, self-perpetuating economy. You could find billiard halls, clothing stores, music shops, furniture stores, confectionaries, meat markets, hotels, restaurants and a movie theater, along with a library, two schools, a hospital and two newspapers.

The Vernon A.M.E. Church was the only building on North Greenwood Avenue to "survive" the massacre. But only the basement and parts of the lower level remained intact. By 1928, the structure had been rebuilt – solely through private donations.

Dell Gines, lead community development advisor for the Federal Reserve Bank of Kansas City's Omaha branch, has called it the best example he knows of a truly inclusive entrepreneurial ecosystem. We have nothing like it today.

Along with the erasure of Black Wall Street came the blotting out of the event itself.

Said the *Times*: "The act of remembering the Tulsa Race Massacre has been smothered, resisted, and contested for the entire century since it took place. For many decades, few spoke of how hordes of white Tulsans with deep racial resentment had stormed Greenwood, one the country's most prosperous Black neighborhoods. Overcoming a fierce defense by those who lived in Greenwood, the mob brutally slaughtered residents before pillaging and burning most of the district to the ground."

Years of forgetting led to years of denial but time also led to the truth, wriggling up deep from its red-dirt burial.

In October 2020, archaeologists found the outlines of at least 10 buried coffins, one of several mass grave sites that historians had long been searching for. The excavations will likely continue and attempts to identify survivors of the exhumed bodies will continue as well.

Faced with massive evidence, it has become next to a impossible to now claim nothing happened. But strangely, the fact that this horrible event did occur seems the only thing everyone here agrees on.

What about the survivors?

Greenwood Rising describes the history center as telling "the specific story of the dignity of a people who turned trials, tribulations, and tragedy into a triumph of the human spirit." Among its recent visitors was Ann Myers, a Tulsa resident.

Oklahoma may stand as the worst location yet for a teaching ban like Gov. Kevin Stitt's

Oklahoma may stand as the worst location yet for a teaching ban like Gov. Kevin Stitt's, which came about after a conservative panic spread nationwide over the graduate-level teaching of critical race theory, a concept that racial bias — intentional or not — is so deeply rooted in U.S. laws and institutions that it leads to differential outcomes by race. The centennial commission summed it up well, saying, "The bill serves no purpose than to fuel the racism and denial that afflicts our communities and our nation."

Before it became a state in 1907, the area served as the transplanted home to Indigenous tribes pushed out of other sections of the country to fulfill the nation's thirst for white settlement and expansion. It also attracted formerly enslaved people fleeing the South. Some Black people had been brought there by slave-holding tribes.

Many of those folks even hoped to make Oklahoma a majority-Black state, free from white terror.

But with the possibility of land, white settlers from the surrounding Confederate states rushed in with their culture of Black inferiority in tow. The state's first law? A Jim Crow statute requiring segregation of railcars and depots. Pulitzer Prize winning author Isabel Wilkerson famously wrote in her book *The Warmth of Other Suns* that even phone booths in Oklahoma were segregated.

Tulsa didn't have an elected Black City Council member until 1990, when the city adopted a ward system.

The racial problems in the city didn't end when the fires from 1921 were extinguished. Reparations often surface as a way to address our legacy racial issues, but opponents typically say they weren't around when the injustice occurred and shouldn't have to pay for it or that there are no survivors to actually pay.

Those excuses fall flat in Tulsa.

Days before the events planned in 2021, the three known survivors of the massacre appeared before a congressional committee to talk about their experiences, to share what they saw that awful day, and to ask for the measure of justice they'd been denied all these decades since. C-SPAN carried their testimony live and re-ran the hearing during the recent Memorial Day holiday.

Even phone booths in Oklahoma were segregated.

Viola Ford Fletcher, now 109, spoke hauntingly about Black people being shot and Black bodies lying in the streets. Her brother, Hughes Van Ellis, then 100, also shared images of what he saw, but his voice began to break. The memories, all these years later, remained painful for him. Lessie Benningfield Randle, then 106, also testified.

Each pressed for reparations.

In so many other debates about racism and how to confront it, the call for reparations has been based on something that happened hundreds of years ago. We're reaching out over centuries and studying disparities, looking for evidence or leafing through old documents in trying to put a puzzle together. But amazingly, here we have centenarian survivors. They are eyewitnesses not just to what happened, but to the aftermath of conscious and willful misremembering.

The Tower of Reconciliation at John Hope Franklin Reconciliation Park in Tulsa gives voice to those died and were brutalized in the Greenwood Massacre while depicting the sweeping history of the African-American struggle. The tower is the work of sculptor Ed Dwight, the first Black man to graduate from Bishop Ward High School in Kansas City, Kansas. Dwight served in the Air Force and might have been a pioneering astronaut but for what he called the "racial politics" of the day. After leaving the service, he has reached new heights in the art world, creating well over 100 large-scale and public art installations.

A cultural center is nice for the public — Blacks and whites — but in and of itself, it could not possibly compensate survivors.

Imagine first, that a society that claims to have granted you full-citizenship status, has chased you out of its mainstream and into its margins and then sets hard boundaries to keep you there. Against all the odds, you build a profitable business and a cozy home for yourself and your family with the half expanse of the sky you've been allotted.

But then, the very society that chased you into the margins, now begrudges you the portion you'd built for yourself and, on the pretense of upholding order, descends violently on your business and your home. Police officers, sheriff's deputies, all manner of "public servants" join in the burning and sacking of your property. Crop dusting planes drop turpentine and tar bombs from the sky.

The public servants and others rob your home and business, carrying off your clothes, your jewelry and other valuables and the fires they set gobble up the rest of your belongings as well as your home.

When the torrent of violence ends, your life in ruins, you're herded into camps and held there by many of the same people who terrorized you for the previous two days. You try seeking justice, but no one in authority cares enough to honor your claims. In fact, a great pall of silence and denial settles over the community, which quickly gets busy forgetting. Decades later, there's hardly a trace of the crimes.

As a century passes, new generations discover the horrors of those deadly days. Denial has given way to angst among the descendants of the apartheid. They still control the municipal government and instead of "no," now you hear excuses about statutes of limitations, about legal standing in lawsuits, about white people feeling uncomfortable with direct payouts.

Some white residents suggest that the new history center was a form of reparations and that the building and its programs should suffice.

Progress?

Despite all that history and all the divisions and the steep learning curve, Goodwin says Tulsans can navigate these narrow and rocky racial straits.

"I'd say first, because the world is looking at Tulsa right now. It's in the public eye. Worldwide. Everyone is watching."

Goodwin says Tulsa is very sensitive about its history and somewhat apologetic about it. It also has a vibrant community fund with a national reputation. It is a source of civic pride, he says, and that pressure of public opinion has the power to nudge residents toward their better angels.

"There are also people of goodwill in Tulsa," Goodwin says.

On the surface, the Tulsa standoff could seem to be about reparations, and even conservative journalist David Brooks of *The New York Times* has said that there must be an effort to address the wide disparities in our culture.

"Reparations and integration are the way to do that," Brooks once wrote. "Reparations would involve an official apology for centuries of slavery and discrimination, and spending money to reduce their effects."

There's also a wrong way to do this, he cautioned.

"Trying to find the descendants of slaves and sending them a check," Brooks said. "That would launch a politically ruinous argument over who qualifies for the money, and at the end of the day people might be left with a $1,000 check that would produce no lasting change."

But that's not the real issue. The real issue, many say, rests in the resentments and resistance about reparations.

Why, many asked, in such a litigious society do we suspend those standards because the plaintiffs are Black? The historical evidence overwhelms. Survivors and witnesses remain. As Americans, we fall heir to the nation's bounties and benefits as well as its debts and obligations. Most of us didn't fight in Korea or Vietnam, but our taxes still flow to those now in retirement who did serve.

We can't pick and choose which line items our taxes will support.

The racial factions can't agree on progress because their respective communities have experienced life in different castes.

Several Tulsans, speaking on background only, accused Greenwood Rising and the centennial commission that birthed it of hollow racial window dressing. They contend that the entity is little more than a symbolic gesture toward people needing concrete change, including but not limited to financial reparations. Many said the museum couldn't possibly replace the loss of homes and businesses.

Is there progress in that the episode is no longer referred to as a "riot"? Sure.

But author James Baldwin may have said it best when he said, "There is scarcely any hope for the American Dream because people who are denied participation in it, by their very presence, will wreck it."

In 1921, the city saw years and years of work to build a stalwart business community destroyed *in a matter of hours*. If the city (as well as the nation) is going to survive, this confrontation with its past must yield more than just new buildings, more tourists and courteous conversations. Like the history that forced its way up from its burial, a long-denied justice must emerge from this work.

It's the real work that begins inside the building, after the construction is complete.

11/ Why Hide our Historical Roots?

January 24, 2022

Forty-five years ago this month, the televised miniseries *Roots,* based on a book written by Alex Haley, uncle of Sen. David Haley (D-Kansas City), premiered. The series reintroduced this nation to a tortured history it has tried to forget.

Few people in America have a more interesting vantage point on critical race theory — or just race — than Sen. Haley and his family.

Roots, which depicted the Haley family's direct lineage, remains one of the most-watched programs in network broadcast history. It traces the journey of the family's ancestor, Kunta Kinte, from capture in West Africa, his harsh transportation across the Atlantic and sale into a lifetime of American slavery. It beamed countless barbarities experienced by people whose lives were so lived because of their race into millions of homes.

Sen. Haley said through this lens, he has viewed the sometimes hysterical debate about critical race theory as a marketing torch igniting fears in a particular voting bloc. Purveyors of these tactics know they work. Americans rarely disappoint racial fear peddlers.

Sen. Haley said he chooses to remember, however, how our country watched his family history unfold over those eight nights. Perhaps for the first time in 100 years, Americans began wrestling with the hidden-away horrors of dividing a society by color. This wasn't simply his family's story, but our national story: America's true history.

"We need this unifying spirit now," Sen. Haley said. "We're losing our sense of empathy as a nation."

Deep learning often happens in discomfort. We heal only after fully acknowledging our history and addressing its legacy. But no one supporting this crusade against honesty in education will address just how our students will be able to study Kansas history.

Sen. Haley had important questions about the classroom repercussions of dodging discussions about America's racial past. He wondered, for example, if prohibitions against racial content would mean teachers couldn't discuss slavery.

"Without slavery, what does Kansas as a 'free state' even mean?" Sen. Haley asked.

He asked if students could read *The Learning Tree*, Gordon Parks' epic work, and discuss the violent racism that drove him from Fort Scott and kept him estranged from the state until late in his life?

And what about literary icon Langston Hughes, who lived in Lawrence? What does the Harlem Renaissance or "New Negro Movement" mean without racial discussions?

Could students discuss John Brown and "Bleeding Kansas?" You know, the guy immortalized in a painting inside the Capitol. The one with the rifle and the Bible and the blazing eyes. Are we supposed to just walk by the mural and pretend we don't know who he is?

**The infamous Kansas abolitionist John Brown as depicted in a
detail of John Steuart Curry's famous "Tragic Prelude" mural in the
Kansas Capitol. (Sherman Smith/Kansas Reflector)**

Sen. Haley also questioned whether the people concerned about CRT would cancel recently departed Bob Dole.

"Sen. Dole knew race mattered," Sen. Haley said. "We know this because of his support for Section 8(A) provisions, which set aside a portion of federal contracts for minority (and later women) business development."

"I also have to wonder if *Roots* itself could even be taught or viewed in classrooms," he said.

Some now propose the historical version of don't ask, don't tell, regarding our racial past. It's a tacit admission that what Black Americans have suffered is so objectionable, it would demand immediate justice. The truth is so resounding, it can never be uttered.

Roots delivered transformative content into American homes. It transformed Sen. Haley, too. He'd just entered Morehouse College, and in a week, he "went from just another freshman to Kunta Kinte's descendant."

It also connected past to present. Black Americans endured and continue to endure disparities in median income, household wealth, life expectancy and more.

White Americans saw this, too, but they winced and looked away.

Given this history, it is understandable, Sen. Haley said, that *Roots* stood a whisker away from the title "Before This Anger." His Uncle Alex, however, wanted *Roots* to speak to the collective pride of Black Americans at how they'd survived such barbarity.

This fear of any racial discussion feels craven. Americans are supposed to face and overcome challenges, not hide from them. But that is what opponents of CRT propose. Deflect Native American history, hide Asian contributions and ignore our Latinx past. Deny any and all antecedent truths.

Many races and cultures helped build this great country.

Sen. Haley rightly asks if we want to send our students into an incredibly diverse society unaware of much of America's history. Aspects of our history are ugly, but our beauty emerges from struggles against such ugliness.

We must choose.

We can continue filtering the past, picking and choosing through the grimy lens of incomplete

Some now propose the historical version of don't ask, don't tell, regarding our racial past. It's a tacit admission that what Black Americans have suffered is so objectionable, it would demand immediate justice.

history, or live up to America's greatest aspirations of honesty and truth.

12/ Kansas Should Market Its Rich Civil Rights History

February 11, 2025

Governor Laura Kelly (D) bracketed by Black legislators and others gathered Feb. 19, 2024, at the Capitol, signed a proclamation marking the historical contributions of Black people to Kansas communities and the ongoing fight for racial justice. (Tim Carpenter/Kansas Reflector)

I took a tour group to Alabama in 2015 to trace the American Civil Rights Trail, running in a triangle from Birmingham to Montgomery to Selma and back to Birmingham.

In Birmingham, we visited the historic 16th Street Baptist Church, where racists killed four little girls dressing for Sunday School. We walked Kelly Ingram Park across the street, where replica water cannons and snarling dogs depicted the Children's Campaign.

In Montgomery, we visited Commerce Street, named for the human beings sold there. We saw Dexter

Avenue Baptist Church, where the Rev. Dr. Martin Luther King Jr. pastored. Not far from the church, we saw the alabaster Confederate Capital, the original seat of the Confederacy.

In Selma, an eyewitness to the Bloody Sunday attack on peaceful civil rights activists showed us the Edmund Pettus Bridge where the beatings began, and the site where segregationists beat three clergymen, including one hailing from Wichita who died two days later from a clubbing to the head. King gave the man's eulogy.

The fact that a monument honors the slain cleric, the Rev. James Reeb, in Selma, left me musing about how little Kansas promotes itself as a destination for Black history enthusiasts, and how we're leaving lots of potential tourist money on the table.

As Plains people, we maintain a certain modesty. We need to get over that. Our history remains incredibly marketable yet untapped.

Think about this.

The 2012 Oscar-winning film *Lincoln*, featuring Daniel Day Lewis, opened with a conversation between Lincoln and two soldiers from the First Kansas Colored.

Kansans played a critical role in the establishment of the Smithsonian's National Museum of African American History and Culture. Then-Sen. Sam Brownback brought the bill in the Senate to establish the museum. The late civil rights icon Rep. John Lewis brought a similar bill in the House.

President George W. Bush appointed my friend Eric Sexton to the charter board for the museum, and Kansas had more people on that board than any other state.

Inside the museum, Kansas history resounds.

A Stearman plane, most likely built in Wichita, hangs from the ceiling. There's a Nicodemus sign featured in an exhibition about Black towns. The Brown v. Board decision is featured in the segregation section, along with items my staff at the Kansas African American Museum submitted about the 1958 Dockum sit-in, the first successful student-led sit-in in the nation's history.

There's also art from Topeka's Aaron Douglass, references to John Brown and "Bleeding Kansas," images of native Wichitan Hattie McDaniel — the first Black person to win an Oscar — and photographs of and by the great Gordon Parks, a native of Fort Scott.

Others seem to value our history more than we do.

A few years ago, while I still worked at the Kansas African American Museum, some historians reached out from the U.N. Educational, Scientific and Cultural Organization, also known as UNESCO. They discussed establishing Topeka as "the western terminus" of an American Civil Rights Trail.

All this, and we've only scratched the surface.

In northeast Kansas, we could have an anchor museum in Quindaro, considered the first and best example of a multi-racial democracy in Kansas or elsewhere. A walking path from Quindaro could simulate the Underground Railroad all the way to Topeka.

In south-central Kansas, there should be a President Barack Obama heritage site because his mom was born there; a larger "Double V" Campaign memorial; and preservation of the old St. Peter Claver Catholic

Church, where Dockum sit-in participants practiced and steeled themselves for their step into history.

We also could expand the Kansas African American History Trail. The original trail was launched by Nicodemus native Angela Bates. Back when I was at the Kansas African American Museum, we wrote a federal grant adding signage that directed tourists to sites across the state, including the Buffalo Soldier Museum, the Ritchie House in Topeka and a John Brown site in Osawatomie.

All this, and we still haven't brushed on Donald Hollowell, born in Wichita but known in Atlanta as "Mr. Civil Rights" for serving clients such as King, Lewis and Julian Bond, and for giving Washington, D.C., powerbroker Vernon Jordan his first job.

Other states would cherish these kinds of historical and cultural opportunities. To whom much is given, much is required, right?

Just because we have history to spare, doesn't mean that we should.

CHALLENGING THE STATUS QUO

13/ Josephine Brown Stood Strong Against Discrimination

January 7, 2026

Josephine Vonceal Pace "Jo" Brown was the first Black woman to chair Wichita's School Board. She died Dec. 31. (Photo by Mark McCormick)

Josephine Vonceal Pace "Jo" Brown visited my high school back in the 1980s. The administration at good ol' North High invited her to speak about her historic career as the first Black woman to chair the Wichita School Board.

We learned that day that Mrs. Jo spoke hard, even painful truths wrapped in her unique brand of sophistication. No one had the status nor the courage to censor her. Her voice carried.

She told the auditorium about the Wichita she'd lived through, including a practice of allowing Black students to swim only late on Fridays, after white students. Staff then drained and refilled the pool, to save white students from swimming in the same water.

That story landed hard. We were the last generation of youth whose parents were shaped in a pre-civil rights America. We understood this historically, but Mrs. Jo made us feel it.

That will moor much of her legacy: standing 10-toes or high-heels down on truth and giving people the kind of cultural equilibrium to speak loud and true about what hurts.

She died New Year's Eve at 96, unwilling to let the year end before having her final say.

Years later, as a columnist, my reference to that pool story in a column ignited a reader firestorm. White, Jim Crow-era graduates claimed that the pools weren't segregated.

Letters begat calls for a retraction and for me to be fired. I dug in as the newspaper brass pressed me to relent.

Enter Mrs. Jo.

"They're after you, aren't they, baby?"

"Yes, ma'am."

She said, "Humph," with a resolve in her voice. The cavalry had arrived.

"Here's what you do," she said. "You go down to the Central Branch Library. Go into the Special Collections desk and ask for a book written by Sandra Van Meter."

Mrs. Jo explained that as board chair, she'd commissioned a book documenting the district's history and that in one of the chapters, we'd all learn the truth, and it proved worse than anything I'd shared.

The district literally had convened discussions about building a separate school to keep Black students and white students out of the same water. The district never built that separate building but maintained the strange water-purity practice.

Similar stories existed from Wichita to Salina to progressive Lawrence and into the South. Heather McGhee, in her 2021 book, *The Sum of Us,* shared how Montgomery, Alabama, paved over its municipal pool — that Black taxes help build — rather than integrate it.

It's precisely this kind of history many Americans today would banish rather than face. Their revulsion at this black-and-white image of themselves offers a brutal contrast to the lived experience of Black residents only allowed to skate or visit dentists on certain days.

Mrs. Jo fought against such practices, and she's partly the reason I prioritize telling various historic and social truths regardless of the often-frightening backlash.

The point was not for her to forever stand behind me but to show me how to stand on my own. Much of the courage I stood on, whether calling out a school bus company or a police website humiliating women, came from her.

Imagine what she lived through, not just as an educator following the *Brown* decision, but in a district that considered foregoing federal funds rather than integrating. Letters from white parents who didn't want "n-words" teaching their children.

Despite that, she offered a warm smile and regal kindness. She never seemed bitter, just resolutely unbothered. When I read this stanza in "Still I Rise"

> *"Does my haughtiness offend you?*
> *Don't you take it awful hard,*
> *'Cause I laugh like I've got gold mines*
> *Diggin' in my own back yard."*

 it reminded me of Mrs. Jo. In a society expecting her to dim her light, Mrs. Jo set the night sky ablaze with searchlights.

 When she confronted the yet lingering vestiges of that era, at a bank or a store, she would correct them as she might one of her tiny students. Firmly but gracefully.

 "You don't pay *and* beg, baby," she told me once.

She could be blunt, but not cruel. Her advice pinched your heart but fixed your vision. She often attributed her ability to speak so boldly to her husband, the late Dr. Val J. Brown Sr., whose medical practice sheltered her from reprisals.

That voice. It bridged eras and will outlast us all. She used that voice to help so many people and guided still more toward finding their own.

14/ Richard Ney, "Attorney for the Damned" in Kansas

January 30, 2024

Richard Ney once gave me a book to read: *Clarence Darrow: Attorney for the Damned.* It spoke powerfully about Darrow's deeply emotional opposition to the death penalty. Darrow fought for clients as though he himself might find himself crammed into a suffocating pine box.

Ney, one of the state's top defense attorneys and one of the few credentialed to handle federal death penalty cases, seemed to fight for his clients similarly. His recent passing means that Kansas and justice has lost one of its most devoted defenders.

I learned about Richard when I managed a team of reporters who covered the police and the courts. Our court reporter mentioned how Richard had been a federal public defender in Hawaii. We met a few times. I remembered his bearing and the bass in his voice, but also his broad, bearded smile.

Years later, he had a client who had come to Kansas for school but hailed from South Central Los Angeles. The client sat in jail facing the death penalty. Ney visited him regularly but believed the youngster needed interaction with someone other than him. So Ney asked if I'd make weekly visits that the young man's family could not. That began my trips to the jail for Richard's client. It also began my journey of getting to know someone I'd already come to admire. I'm guessing Richard asked me to do the visits because he knew the case would take a while, and he cared about the young man's mind and spirit. I think I'd only visited the jail one other time, but I found myself there once or twice a week.

I never discussed the case with the client. I was there to help him feel human. We talked about his life in L.A., a place I'd grown familiar with as a kid and preteen, with my father and my sister living out there. He talked about sports. He was trying to maintain a long-distance relationship.

The more I learned about the young man, the more I panicked imagining him being killed, guilty or not. I already believed that our system had proven itself incapable of dispensing justice impartially. I had a sense for why Richard always seemed so serious and so resolute, and why he worked so hard.

That client owes Richard his life. Richard didn't win an acquittal, but he got the death penalty taken off the table and the prison sentence pared way down.

According to his obituary, Richard came to Wichita in 1984 and launched the public defender's office. He was the first Kansas lawyer to "successfully introduce testimony given under hypnosis while winning an acquittal for Bill Butterworth, charged with killing three people in a 1987 murder case." His office also was the first to successfully use the battered-woman defense in Sedgwick County.

He was instrumental in broadening the reach of jury selection beyond voter registration rolls, adding driver's licenses. He saw almost daily how prosecutors regularly dismissed Black jurors and felt compelled to try to address that issue.

Richard had John Henry's work ethic, even as modernity marveled at how this locomotive of a man chugged along in all his mundane and disciplined greatness. You knew you'd get his best effort and argument — and yet, he still impressed.

I wrote a series of columns about a stabbing death at a convenience store in which patrons walked around and stepped over the mortally wounded woman. One customer, police said, even paused above the woman and snapped a photo. Richard ended up representing the defendant.

Covering the trial, I thought while watching him work that he'd put up an amazing defense in such a case that had so much pretrial publicity. He really was something to see in court. The so-called "damned" had a zealous advocate in him. Richard Ney earned a degree in journalism from the vaunted Missouri School of Journalism, so in many ways, he and I marched in the same tribe — the journalism tribe, the one where we learn to comfort the afflicted and to afflict the comfortable while scouring landscapes for the best obtainable version of the truth.

He went to law school only to become a better journalist, graduating from the Boston University School of Law and then working as an investigative reporter and editor before moving on to work in public defender offices in Illinois and Vermont.

Richard and his wife Judith had six children. In fact, one of his kids courageously confronted some other kids who bullied my son. I also remember considering moving to my current employer, the American Civil Liberties Union of Kansas, and calling Richard to ask what he knew about the organization.

Sadly, as in many cases of loss, I had not realized all the ways our lives intersected until his passing. Only a few months ago, our national office and our affiliate mounted an argument against the death penalty in district court in Wichita. A court observer recognized me from my visits to Richard's office and shared that

Richard Ney was in the building. He was talking to one of the judges, and I might be able to catch him. I lingered hoping to see him, but somehow I missed him that day. I'm sure a lot of us will.

85

15/ Lassiter Saunders Fights for Transparency

February 26, 2025

If you care about government transparency, particularly in cases of deadly police shootings, LaRonna Lassiter Saunders is a hero.

As *Kansas Reflector* reported this month, lawyers for the city of Topeka and five police officers named in a wrongful-death lawsuit urged a federal magistrate to publicly admonish Lassiter Saunders for disclosing body camera footage of the 2022 shooting of Taylor Lowery.

Worse, the lawyers asked the federal court to compel Lassiter Saunders or the plaintiffs to pay defendants' legal fees for the lawyers' work participating in a court hearing on the issue and preparing the brief demanding sanctions. You read that right. They want the grieving family of the man they shot 34 times to pay their legal fees.

If anything more sinister was ever created, the devil kept it for himself.

Shawnee County District Attorney Mike Kagay opened the door to release of the footage when he issued an erroneous report exonerating the officers. He's the poster child for why citizens need to demand greater transparency and access to police bodycam footage. I reached out to the city of Topeka for comment, but spokeswoman Rosie Nichols said because this matter involves pending litigation, the city would respond through the legal process, and not the news media.

They want the grieving family of the man they shot 34 times to pay their legal fees.

"Law enforcement officers face dangerous and unpredictable situations every day, risking their lives and mental well-being to provide safety and protection to our community," Nichols said. "We will continue to vigorously defend our officers in this matter."

I find the city's comments about not trying this case in the news media hypocritical considering the current request that Lassiter Saunders be publicly admonished for sharing important footage of the shooting with reporters. She's not a member of the Topeka Police Department, but she deserves some kind of protection.

This began in October 2022, when a family member called police out of concern for Lowery's mental health. At the time, Lowery was carrying a knife. Topeka police responded and the video shows that in each interaction with officers, Lowery ran, eventually jumping in a vehicle and driving away. Police followed him to a convenience store parking lot, where several officers confronted Lowery who had dropped both the knife and a wrench.

At least one officer shoved Lowery, an indication that they weren't concerned about the wrench in that moment.

Surrounded by officers with their guns drawn, Lowery reached for the wrench on the ground and moved away from officers as they began firing. Officers shot at him 34 times. The knife was clearly visible at the feet of one of the officers as the group fired.

It was Kagay who released information furthering the narrative in TPD and Kansas Bureau of Investigation news releases that Lowery ran at officers with a knife over his head, an impossible characterization for anyone who has seen the video.

Had Lassiter Saunders not shared the video with reporters, Kagay's mischaracterizations would have continued unchallenged. After a possible settlement, the city and DA likely would seek a nondisclosure agreement. Poof, the video would disappear.

Concerned about how this bungled situation would play publicly, Kagay and the city of Topeka now want to shift the spotlight from their behavior onto Lassiter Saunders.

I reached Lassiter Saunders for comment, but she declined, and I understood.

Had Lassiter Saunders not shared the video with reporters... Poof, the video would disappear.

Defense counsel Jeffrey Kuhlman and Nicholas Jefferson have claimed she violated a protective order establishing rules for release of police video tracking movements of Lowery and Topeka police officers Malcolm Gillum, Justin Good, Bradley Netherton, Sgt. Scott McEntire, and Detective Alex Wall during the 2022 episode. U.S. Magistrate Judge Angel Mitchell's December order blocked public release of personally identifiable information of certain witnesses and segments of video containing images of minors. *Kansas Reflector* is not subject to the judge's order and didn't publish the shielded video content.

Mitchell authorized the release of the video, seemingly moved by the argument about the public's interest in seeing the footage.

The lawyers argued Lassiter Saunders' motive for sharing the video was "to try this case in the court of public opinion and to improperly influence and taint the jury pool." That's always the argument when video emerges of law enforcement making deadly mistakes. From their standpoint, there's rarely a reason to release bodycam footage.

But attempts to keep the video secret and then trying to punish Lassiter Saunders aren't about preserving a jury pool. They are about hiding the truth.

I've said repeatedly that we don't begin to arrive at truth until suffering begins to speak.

That's what Lassiter Saunders did. She allowed suffering to begin to speak.

We must categorically reject ploys designed to hide truth from the public. The public has an intense interest in seeing unfiltered, unedited footage of citizens being killed by officers, supposedly in the public interest.

When officers do something heroic — and that happens often — those videos run on a loop on television and online, which tells me that law enforcement tends to release video when it suits them. That should not be the standard. As the Rev. Martin Luther King Jr. once said, quoting James Russell Lowell: "Truth forever on the scaffold, wrong forever on the throne." The quote continues: "Yet that scaffold sways the future. Behind the dim unknown stands God within the shadows, keeping watch above His own."

People desperately trying to hide the truth want her on the scaffold.

The Topeka community and everyone who cares about transparency in deadly police shootings should rally around Lassiter Saunders. People desperately trying to hide the truth want her on the scaffold.

16/ Hummingbird Made of Steel: Jeannie Eblen

November 23, 2021

Jeannie Kyger Eblen was known as a "newsroom mom" to KU students who worked at the University Daily Kansan while her husband, Tom (right), was general manager. But that was only one aspect of her energetic life. (Courtney Eblen McCain)

Jeannie Kyger Eblen could never get enough books or magazines, always sought more knowledge on any subject and saw no end to her curiosity. She moved through life like a darting hummingbird — one made of steel.

Jeannie wanted to know what you had to say. And she was so well read that whatever the subject, she likely knew something about it.

Those of us who knew her will miss her terribly. She died suddenly Nov. 11. She was 77.

Jeannie was small, but not delicate; brilliant, but unpretentious; kind, but no pushover. She wore a pixie cut and rimmed glasses and had a dynamite smile. She didn't weigh a thing but could fill a room.

But she also kept a hard hat in her trunk, always seemed to have a screwdriver or wrench handy, and during the winter, wore heavy Carhartt bib overalls and snow boots.

She explored constantly.

She once served as an election judge. She completed the Lawrence police academy for citizens. She even accompanied her daughter Courtney Eblen McCain, then a Texas paramedic, on one of her shifts.

"She enjoyed riding along with me," Courtney said, adding that her mom signed the waiver and donned the required black shoes, black pants, and a white shirt.

Courtney said her endlessly curious mother also had read — cover to cover — her copy of a fire engineer magazine, once asking about the suppression measures firefighters had used to contain a fire on a call Courtney had made.

"She tended to remember everything she read," Courtney said. "I'd say, 'Well, Mom, I was working on the medical part of that run, so I don't know.'"

Jeannie subscribed to the *Tulsa Jewish Review,* not because she was Jewish — she wasn't — but because she found faith interesting. She read a lot about the world's religions, from Buddhism, Hinduism, Islam, and more.

> *Jeannie was small, but not delicate; brilliant, but unpretentious; kind, but no pushover.*

She also read *Field and Stream*. She just wanted the knowledge.

"She has tens of thousands of books in this house," Courtney said, "and I suspect she's read all of them."

Courtney considers her mother a trailblazer. At a time when the professional horizons of women consisted largely of nursing or teaching, Jeannie majored in journalism at Oklahoma State University. She moved to Kansas City, where she worked for *The Star* from 1966 to 1976.

According to her obituary, she won a slew of awards, including a Dorothy Dawe Award for home furnishings writing. She also served as the Kansas City field editor for *Better Homes and Gardens*.

I met her through her husband of 51 years, Tom Eblen, the beloved general manager of the *University Daily Kansan* at the William Allen White School of Journalism. She would sit with me at WAW functions, helping me feel welcome. She lovingly embraced Tom's students as their "newsroom mom."

Jill Jess, the former news director at KU, once worked with Jeannie there.

"She was a super quick study on everything," Jess said. "She could master any computer program."

But then a wave of budget cuts claimed Jeannie's hometown news specialist job, Jess said. She and university relations director Todd Cohen had to tell her.

"How do you lay off your 'mom'?" Jess asked. "We felt so awful. She ended up comforting us."

Jeannie lovingly cared for Tom as his health declined. She was his caregiver for about six years. He died in 2017.

In recent years, she waged a private battle with lymphoma. It didn't slow her down.

"It just became something she added to her to-do list," Courtney said. "There was a lot of 'stiff upper lip' in our family. You can sit here and whine about it, or you can get up and get it done. That's how my brother and I were raised."

The pandemic proved more formidable.

"She couldn't go to her museums," Courtney said. "She couldn't visit her grandchildren. I couldn't be around her when she was immune-suppressed."

But, she made do.

She read the usual number of newspapers she subscribed to every day. She chatted with her grandchildren on Zoom. She made her home her castle.

She grew up on a farm in southeast Kansas. There were no repairmen. You didn't order pizza. You did for yourself, or it didn't get done.

For Jeannie, there was always more to do.

17/ Kansan Arthur Fletcher, the "Father of Affirmative Action"

August 21, 2022

The Supreme Court will take up the issue of affirmative action in a pair of student admission cases asking the court to overturn its 2003 decision in *Grutter v. Bollinger*, which upheld the University of Michigan's practice of considering race in its undergraduate admissions process to diversify its student body.

The Harvard case questions whether the university has violated the Civil Rights Act by capping Asian American student admissions. Considering that we may remember this court as one of the most hostile ever to African American civil rights, affirmative action is likely on its last leg.

That's sad, considering that the man a national newspaper called the "father of affirmative action," Arthur Fletcher, grew up here in Kansas. Many of his struggles remain struggles for Black Americans, long after his lifetime of work to make things better.

I first learned about Fletcher from my mentor, the famed Wichita architect Charles McAfee. I eventually wrote a column about his life and that column appears in my 2017 book, *Some Were Paupers, Some Were Kings*, published by Blue Cedar Press.

Fletcher devised a plan forcing Philadelphia construction companies working under federal contracts to establish minority hiring goals and to make good-faith progress on those goals or face

Arthur Fletcher, who was once called the "Father of Affirmative Action," grew up in Kansas. (U.S. Department of Labor)

substantial penalties. He was Nixon's assistant labor secretary in the 1960s.

People pilloried the plan, criticizing its reliance on counting and quotas, but it became a model for similar programs nationwide.

"We have no problem counting who's on welfare, we have no problem counting who's in jail, we have no problem counting who's on (Aid to Families with Dependent Children)," Fletcher, a trailblazing Black Republican, once told *The Wichita Eagle.* "What's wrong with counting success?"

Indeed.

Success in that case meant a fairer distribution of access and opportunity, something that these admission policies under scrutiny by the high court mean to address.

It only seems fair that universities be allowed to use race as one factor in their decision-making.

U.S. House Education and Labor Committee Chairman Bobby Scott of Virginia recently filed a brief along with 64 other House Democrats urging the Supreme Court to uphold a college or university's ability to factor race into college admission processes.

"Even with the use of a race-conscious admissions program, the University of North Carolina (UNC) 'continues to face challenges admitting and enrolling underrepresented minorities, particularly African American males, Hispanics, and Native Americans,'" the group wrote.

That underrepresentation isn't accidental. It is the direct result of centuries of policy and custom. No fewer than 12 generations of Black people endured state-sanctioned and state-sponsored discrimination and terror.

These terrors — physical, financial and psychological — are the offspring of our racial caste system, and they persist today. Our wealth gaps, our health disparities, our school achievement gaps and the continuous spate of extra-judicial killings of unarmed Black people by police fit neatly inside our racial caste system.

Fletcher eventually advised four U.S. presidents: Nixon, Ford, Reagan and George H.W. Bush. He served as the deputy assistant for urban affairs and as the chairman of the Civil Rights Commission.

But years earlier, when he played football, three teams in the Big Six Conference wouldn't play a team with a Black athlete.

He couldn't teach here in Kansas, despite a degree, because that could mean possibly instructing white girls. He attended Washburn University on the G.I. Bill but couldn't live in on-campus G.I. housing.

He graduated and played pro football, but no white employer would hire him, so he got a job delivering ice.

"I'm a college graduate ice man, and the joke of the town," he once said in a *Wichita Eagle* interview.

Cases such as the one the court will hear soon emerge in an existence undisturbed by the kind of ugliness Fletcher and other Black people experienced and continue to confront. Yet people will stand in front of the high court and with a straight face claim race no longer matters in this society.

In a statement reported last week by *Kansas Reflector*, Congressman Scott said it well: "Narrowly tailored admissions policies that recognize race as one criterion — out of many criteria for evaluating prospective students — are a key tool to realize diverse learning environments and address continued educational inequity."

Interestingly, Fletcher is credited with coining the phrase, "A mind is a terrible thing to waste," for the United Negro College Fund. His life taught him much about opportunities and success. He was right.

We should be able to count successes as well as challenges.

It only seems fair that universities be allowed to use race as one factor in their decision-making.

Especially when police, voter suppressors, prosecutors, juries, bank loan officers and many others already regularly do this in their dealings with Black people.

18/ Kansas Rep. Gail Finney, the Best Kind of Warrior

September 1, 2022

Wichita Democratic Rep. Gail Finney, right, died Aug. 20 at age 63. Columnist Mark McCormick says her example should inspire Medicaid expansion. (Sherman Smith/Kansas Reflector)

If you knew Wichita Rep. Gail Finney at all, you likely knew her from her work in the Kansas Legislature trying to help people with suspended driver's licenses, trying to help children trapped in our foster care system, trying to get the state's utility company to remove 105-foot towers from people's front yards.

Her servant leadership set her apart. She really seemed to take her constituents' needs and hardships to heart. Sadly, she died Aug. 20 at 63.

In her memory, Kansans should expand Medicaid. She fought for the policy, and it offers a great way to honor such a great and honorable person. This wouldn't be a new fight, but her name and reputation can give it renewed purpose and focus.

Gail loved to laugh. She used to put out a magazine. She loved history. She also produced a Black Expo. In the Legislature, she pushed legalization of medical marijuana, the restoration of classroom funding, returning to annual state budgeting and revisiting tax credits.

But more than anything, the issue that might have been closest to her heart was Medicaid expansion.

Kansas Gov. Laura Kelly has pushed this idea during her administration, aiming to provide more than 150,000 Kansans with access to affordable health care. The measure also would create more than 23,000 new jobs, helping to shore up the Kansas economy.

"It's time to work together to deliver for Kansans and get this done once and for all," Kelly said, according to the *Kansas Reflector*. "Expansion would inject billions of dollars into our state, create thousands of jobs, help retain our health care workers in Kansas and help rural hospitals' bottom lines."

When Gail died, Kelly described her aptly as a "warrior."

Gail proved to be the best kind of warrior, too. Not a weekend warrior, but the daily kind who never worried about the size of the opponent, only the depth of her constituents' need. She took on the biggest, toughest opponents with the same focused tenacity that she brought to any task.

What you may not have known was how she suffered from illnesses and chronic pain, and how difficult it was for her to finally get that kidney transplant she needed. This gave her willingness to pick up a sword and shield and enter political arenas as often as she did even greater grandeur.

She likely did her best work in pain and agonizingly fatigued. Don't let her smile and her glam fool you. Gail was tough.

But the fight for expansion in this state, and the fight for universal health care nationally, also have proven extraordinarily tough.

An August 2019 story in *New York Times Magazine*, titled "Why doesn't the United States have universal health care? The answer has everything to do with race," argued that America's brutal brand of "low-road capitalism" and its racial caste system routinely thwarted such efforts.

The article draws a line roughly from the end of the Civil War to today. A 2019 book, *Dying of Whiteness: How the Politics of Racial Resentment is Killing America's Heartland*, makes similar arguments. Many Americans would rather die than share health care with "undeserving" people.

But expansion benefits everyone. In fact, it likely would help the red, rural areas that seem most opposed to the measure. If the pandemic taught us anything, it was just how interconnected we remain despite efforts of a powerful minority to maintain an arbitrary separateness and to hoard resources.

Dr. Martin Luther King Jr. called health care injustice inhuman.

Well, Gail fought on this front with her trademark dignity and the effortless way she rose above pettiness. Politicians like Bill Clinton turned the phrase "I feel your pain" into a cliche, but I'd never heard anyone question Gail's sincerity as she advocated for her constituents.

We shouldn't allow our loved ones to dissolve into piles of meaningless papers and documents once they die. We should try to fashion some enduring meaning from their lives and assemble our memories of them into colorful mosaics of purpose.

Hopefully, one of her legislative colleagues picks up this cause, affixes her name to a bill and rallies expansion support statewide and across party lines. Sometimes, important issues need a face to help close the emotional distance on matters that are practical but come with tons of wonky detail.

Gail deserves the recognition, and as she said, so many Kansans need and deserve the coverage.

19/ Kansas' Barry Sanders: Black Talent Still Overlooked

August 27, 2023

Barry Sanders offers a pregame pep talk to high school football students at the Shine Bowl last month in Hays. (Mark McCormick/Kansas Reflector)

Despite Barry Sanders averaging 30 yards a carry in his first three games as a receiver at our Wichita high school, head coach Dale Burkholder said the athletic director warned him not to start Barry at running back.

But for Burkholder's advocacy — defiantly starting Barry at running back and then producing a highlight reel and shopping it to universities — Barry might have found his own dreams deferred.

Coaches, athletic directors and governing organizations exercise tremendous authority — sometimes petty or vindictive — over the dreams of prep athletes. Even Barry nearly fell victim. This story surfaces in the 20th anniversary edition of Barry's book and in a new documentary from NFL Films and Amazon.

The film covers Barry's life beyond football. The book, *Barry Sanders: Now You See Him*, will update readers on his life since retirement at 31. I was its co-author. We grew up on the same street a block apart. Both drop in November, a couple of months after the Detroit Lions unveil Barry's new statue outside Ford Field.

Still, Barry's story almost didn't happen.

"It's amazing to me the fine line between becoming an all-time great athlete, maybe the greatest running back to ever play football, and also never playing your sport professionally," said Paul Monusky, senior producer for NFL Films. "If Barry Sanders' high school coach doesn't ignore the noise and viewpoint of his predecessor, then Barry probably winds up with a completely different life. Every football fan that has ever enjoyed a Barry Sanders run in Stillwater or in Detroit owes a debt of gratitude to coach Burkholder."

Coach B became our coach when our previous coach, Bob Shepler, became athletic director. Shepler, like most of Barry's coaches, considered him too small. Worse, Shepler read Barry's frenetic running style as one driven by fear rather than talent.

Shepler ordered Coach B to start a younger but larger player at running back and move Barry to receiver. Coach B acquiesced but saw what everyone later would see: supernova talent.

When he told Shepler he intended to move Barry to running back, Shepler threatened his job.

But Barry roared in his debut, rushing for 274 yards and four touchdowns and another 50 yards receiving. Officials stopped the game to check Barry's jersey. Defenders claimed Barry had smeared Vaseline on his jersey.

Barry finished the season averaging 10.2 yards per carry. Despite that, few recruiters showed interest. Coach B, recently inducted into the Shrine Bowl Hall of Fame with Barry, produced a highlight tape and wore out shoe leather advocating for Barry.

Finally, an Oklahoma State University assistant who was recruiting Joel Fry, a lineman from our team who was also a scholar and wrestler, asked: Who was that running through your blocks?

The rest was history, but in part, an ugly history.

It took Wichita longer to integrate than many Southern cities. The school board considered foregoing federal funds rather than integrating. Black athletes from that era said white coaches allowed only a few Black players on teams.

In February, I wrote about a prep basketball player who'd been racially harassed at school (depicted as a thick-lipped gorilla in a PowerPoint) and wanted to transfer. He petitioned an all-white Kansas State High School Athletic Association panel that denied his request.

After that article, several Black parents recounted similar encounters with KSHAA.

In a situation likely reported here for the first time, Wichita Collegiate School basketball coach Mitch Fiegel was recorded a few years ago trashing a biracial former player and his family. The caller claimed to be a Georgetown University assistant basketball coach.

"But deep down, do I believe he's a good kid from a good family?" Fiegel said in the recording. "I wouldn't touch that family with a 10-foot pole."

Nathan Washer, head of school at Collegiate, said in a statement that the school had been made aware of the recording "a number of years ago" and that because of an employee confidentiality policy, Fiegel would not be made available for comment.

He added that the coach expressed regret and so did Collegiate leadership.

"Coach Fiegel is clear in his regret for the unfortunate term he used," Washer said in an email exchange. "As a school, we also regret the words used by our coach. But in making decisions on an individual in our employment, we take into account the entire scope of their work over, in this case, three decades of employment."

Washer also said via email: "We have a policy that all media enquiries of this nature must only be with the Head of School," adding that "we do not share the details around an internal investigation concerning any of our employees. What I can say is that we considered all the facts and Mitch Fiegel remains as an employee."

Tuition at Georgetown is about $60,000 a year. Fiegel seemed willing to destroy a kid's opportunity over petty pride. The youngster, the coach's former player, had a good playoff game against him and bowed defiantly in front of the coach on the bench.

Coaches and athletic directors should not have this kind of negative influence over a kid's future. But for Coach B, this might have happened to Barry.

Shepler died in 2014, at age 85. He coached North's football team from 1964-74 and then from 1978 to 1984. His win total left him ranked sixth in City League wins, and he led our school into the playoffs six times. He served as athletic director for nearly 20 years before retiring in 1991.

In fairness to Shepler, no one had seen anything like Barry before. Shepler was old school and wanted Barry to run the play as called rather than improvise.

But Black genius often gets overlooked in our culture, and the consequences are greater for Black athletes who tend to have fewer resources and fewer opportunities.

Barry really was something to see — if you could actually see him. That proved challenging without instant replay. The fleeting glimpses of Barry's genius were almost just that: fleeting.

Despite his talent, our flawed prep football system that had difficulty acknowledging Black talent — a system still firmly in place — nearly accomplished what a decade's worth of college and pro defenses could not: stopping him.

Barry really was some- thing to see — if you could actually see him. That proved challenging without instant replay.

20/ William "Buggs" Polite: Undaunted Public Servant

May 1, 2025

Wichita native William "Buggs" Polite smiles for a photo on his birthday. (Mark McCormick)

When I learned that William "Buggs" Polite, one of my oldest friends and a person I deeply admired from my old neighborhood, had died following a stroke, my thoughts turned to Ta-Nehisi Coates' 2015 masterpiece, *Between the World and Me*.

In one passage, Coates discussed losing his friend and classmate Prince Jones. Buggs wasn't young, but to many of us, he was every bit the prince, and one who'd long been denied his crown. Buggs experienced the plunder of opportunities so common for Black professionals.

Still, he continually gave and continually served.

"I would smile whenever I saw him," Coates wrote of his friend, "for I felt the warmth when I was around him and was slightly sad when the time came to trade dap and for one of us to go."

That passage suits Buggs, the quintessential example of the good person you wanted good fortune to bless.

Buggs was a fixture of my childhood.

Playing 21 on a homemade goal behind Tony Hill's house. Tackle the Man football along Don Eaton's red duplex. Bumper pool and basketball pickup games at the MEFSEC (Moving Effectively for Social and Economic Change), now the Lynette Woodard Center.

Buggs stood out. He didn't bully us. He seemed interested in what us little kids said. He encouraged us. I remember playing an entire summer of baseball and him smiling there in his bowlegged stance, at the last game of the season, after I swatted my one and only hit.

At North High, Buggs blazed trails.

One of our beloved counselors, Tommie Williams, bragged about how Buggs posted a near-perfect ACT score, and that Buggs had broken the classroom barrier of a teacher who'd said Black students couldn't excel in his class.

He wrote an insightful editorial for the *North Star* newspaper, explaining how men wearing an earring could symbolize ties to African culture. He launched "B-BASE," or Blacks for Better Academics and Social Equality.

Buggs then headed east to Atlanta's historic Morehouse College, the school that accepted Martin Luther King Jr. when King was only 15. Buggs majored in math and eventually led charter schools. He once worked for one of basketball icon Magic Johnson's foundations.

That meant little when he returned to Wichita and applied for a leadership position at a neighborhood youth center. We were shocked and angry when he wasn't chosen. He was one of our brightest stars.

You might expect someone so accomplished to join in the orgy of self-promotion that seems so commonplace, but I don't remember him ever bragging, even though he was one of the few who justifiably could. He wanted that job. I sensed his disappointment.

I'd once written an article about the city's Black brain drain. Famed architect Charles McAfee inspired the article. He said our segregated community produced numerous PhDs who were forced to leave Wichita to find opportunity.

That's theft. That's plunder. Too often, our hometown served as a killing field for Black professionals' dreams. I felt that was a crown that had been denied him.

Undaunted, Buggs continued to give, and he eventually gained his crown as a stalwart in the public school system.

He tutored kids in math. He and Hercules Finley visited incarcerated youths and encouraged them. Buggs secured a building allowing him to expand his vision. He excitedly raised money and the hopes of community youths.

"The thing to understand about Prince Jones is that he exhibited the whole of his given name," Coates wrote. "He was kind. Generosity radiated off him, and he seemed to have a facility with everyone and everything. This can never be true, but there are people who pull the illusion off without effort, and Prince was one of them."

Buggs, too.

A lasting image of him came after my mother's funeral. I had just slipped Pastor Lincoln Montgomery folded bills through a handshake as my family patriarch instructed, and there stood Buggs, his face registering the hurt and concern you'd expect from a friend.

"There are people," Coates said, "whom we do not fully know, and yet they live in a warm place within us, and when" we lose them, "and the dark energy disperses, that place becomes a wound."

This wound, for me and for that community, will take years to heal.

CHALLENGES NOW

21/ The On-Going Fight after Historic Abortion Vote

September 11, 2022

The busloads of men I had accompanied as a journalist to 1995's Million Man March seemed stunned by the news media count of only 400,000 men on Washington, D.C.'s mall the previous day. I wrote that journalists at the march must have used the three-fifths compromise in calculating the size of the crowd.

Aerial estimates put attendance between 800,000 and 1.2 million.

U.S. Rep. Sharice Davids, right, embraced Kansas Senate Minority Leader Dinah Sykes at an Aug. 2 primary election watch party in Overland Park. Davids won reelection to a third term Tuesday by defeating Republican Amanda Adkins. (Lily O'Shea Becker/Kansas Reflector)

The idea of counting a human being as three-fifths human has its own horrors, but at least we were counted. Women don't appear in the U.S. Constitution. Their unenumerated existence explains for some why guns have more rights than the women in our lives.

The historic vote Aug. 2, however, could mark the beginning of the end of the systematic erasure of women in this nation. Kansas women likely looked at the results of the vote and wondered if there was anything they *couldn't* do.

Voter registration zoomed by 1,000%, according to news reports in the weeks leading up to the special election, and more than 60% of those registrations were women. The resulting tidal wave of turnout helped Kansans turn back an effort to turn the clock back on women and their right to govern their own bodies.

Of course, abortion to many people isn't so cut and dried. There's nuance, they say. Complexities.

But leaning too much into those "complexities" likely would require a violation of a woman's agency to decide if she wants to become a parent or not. We were facing the probability of the government forcing women to carry pregnancies to term.

Almost simultaneously, many Kansans bitterly and angrily fought mandatory masking measures during the pandemic, considering such a request as tyranny. No way we men will ever find our bodies managed and directed the way society seems to want to do for women.

Women having these intimate, personal rights put up for a public vote was wrong in the first place.

Frankly, women having these intimate, personal rights put up for a public vote was wrong in the first place. Inalienable rights shouldn't fall subject to the tyranny of the majority. It was wrong for women to have to turn out in droves to defend a right they should already enjoy.

It felt as though draconian restrictions on contraception and prying, criminal investigations into any miscarriage would follow on the heels of this vote were it successful. The whole situation was terrifying.

But these efforts aren't new.

I remember the national push during the 1970s to pass the Equal Rights Amendment. Even as a child, I understood that women deserved equal rights. I couldn't understand why people considered this effort controversial. But controversial it was. It didn't pass.

One of my co-workers once shared that there was a time when she couldn't have her own credit card. She could only carry one with her husband's name.

In the recent HBO documentary *The Janes,* about a group of Chicago women who pioneered abortion services in the 1960s, women said they couldn't receive birth control unless they were married. Many bought dime store rings and called them "Mrs. (made-up husband's name)" to get the care they sought.

I once interviewed the trailblazing entrepreneur Xavia Hightower, who ran two mortuaries in two Kansas cities. To get a loan, her bank insisted that she needed a husband to manage her affairs. So, she married a man to come to the bank with her, and she continued running her business.

I've barely scratched the absurdities women have had to deal with.

Even in the issue of police terror, we aren't affording women's voices the attention they deserve.

How often have you read about police departments losing rape kits? How seriously do we take the issue of stalking? And in recent years with the spate of the killing of unarmed Black men, it appears that police officers are sexually assaulting women at alarming rates during traffic stops. There's a federal investigation into this matter right now in Kansas City, Kansas.

Maybe that's why, for many Kansas women and women across the nation, the Aug. 2 "no" vote felt worthy of a Helen Reddy primal roar.

That vote indeed should mark a new beginning.

A beginning for women to add themselves to the American mosaic, where for so long, men and their accomplices simply painted over them.

22/ Consequences for All from Treating Suspects as Subhuman

October 22, 2024

My junior high school world history teacher once explained to us how our government prepared the American public for the grotesqueries of war. First, he said, the government had to reduce the enemy to "thing" status, spreading racist names and caricatures of the Japanese and Germans in World War II.

My university African studies professor described a similar process pertaining to Africans stolen from their continent and transformed into a kind of fuel that powered this nation into a world economic power. He called it "reification." This is innocence maintenance.

These old lessons exploded in my mind recently in a rising, fiery curl when a Memphis jury returned terrifying verdicts convicting officers not for kicking and beating Tyree Nichols to death, but for lying about it.

The legal process has not yet run its course. More courtroom days lay ahead.

But that chilling verdict suggests that police can yank motorists from cars, kick and beat them to death — on camera — and half of the public still will say, "go and sin no more." That verdict feels more inhuman than the beating to which Nichols ultimately succumbed.

The jury, six Black people, two Asian people, and eight white people, split on this issue. One portion wanted to convict on the harshest counts, while the other would only convict on the obstruction counts.

It reminded me of the Simi Valley jury that repeatedly watched video of the 1991 police beating of Rodney King and bought the defense's narrative that King, not the officers, controlled that situation. Even the police chief called the officers' behavior excessive.

King survived but suffered a busted leg, a slashed and swollen face, and burns to his chest where police blasted him with a stun gun. He was struck in the face with a billy club.

The jury acquitted three of the officers, but the verdict on the fourth rang with a dismal similarity: not guilty of excessive force and filing a false report, hung jury on count of assault, assault charge dismissed once federal charges were filed.

Two of the officers eventually served two-year, federal prison terms. As a journalist, I've heard greater outcries over the mistreatment of dogs. That's "reification." Reducing humans to a status below dogs.

I can remember a time when beatings such as these went largely unpunished. We've reached a point where some officers, usually racial minorities or women, do occasionally face charges and convictions. Not so much, however, with white male officers. White men still dominate law enforcement, and in professions where white men predominate — cops and district attorneys, for example — they enjoy less accountability.

Having evaded conviction on the most serious charges, most of those officers may find another

The Topeka officers involved in the ... death of Taylor Lowery, who was shot 34 times while holding a wrench, are still working.

department offering them a badge and a gun, and a fresh start in policing.

Can't happen here?

The Topeka officers involved in the October 2023 death of Taylor Lowery, who was shot 34 times while holding a wrench, are still working. One of those officers, Malcolm Gillum, transferred to another law enforcement agency.

Sheila Albers read a *Kansas Reflector* column I'd written about Lowery and reached out to the Kansas Commission on Peace Officer Standards and Training seeking information about Gillum. She said he now works in Shawnee County, where his father retired.

"After reading your story, I sent an open records request on Sept. 17," Albers said in a phone interview. "He started off in the Wabaunsee County Sheriff's Office in June of 2020 to 2022. And then in 2022, he went to Topeka and worked there until June of 2024 when he went to the Shawnee County Sheriff's Office."

What did this mean? Three departments in about four years is a red flag, she said.

"He took a pay cut to go from Topeka to Shawnee," she said. "Why would someone, doing the same work in the same area, leave and take a similar job for less money?"

Albers has learned, painfully, how the Kansas legal system works, or doesn't.

In 2018, Overland Park police officer Clayton Jenison killed her 17-year-old son, John, responding to a potential suicide report. Jenison resigned and the city in 2019 settled a lawsuit with Albers for $2.3 million, according to KCUR.

As if that weren't enough, Johnson County District Attorney Steve Howe issued a false news release a month after the shooting. A 2022 report by the U.S. Justice Department, based on police dash cam video, contradicted Howe's account. Albers filed a complaint accusing Howe of violating a professional conduct rule prohibiting attorneys from making false statements.

The complaint was dismissed, but Howe was "cautioned." The committee "did not find her complaint to be meritless."

Topeka lawyer LaRonna Lassiter Saunders had raised similar questions about comments Shawnee County District Attorney Mike Kagay made about the Lowery shooting.

It's become increasingly clear that unless officers can kill an occasional perp in the regular course of policing, officers will leave for other departments or leave the field altogether.

My brother, Andre Jackson, lives in Memphis and believes the root of the problems there began when that department gutted police salaries and pensions.

"Many senior officers on the force retired or relocated to precincts who were aggressively recruiting with more competitive wages and benefits," Andre said. "What resulted was a void in experienced leadership. Memphis, in a desperate attempt to fill the MPD ranks, pushed candidates through the academy with rushed urgency. The lack of training, discipline, and oversight combined with the high rates of violent crime in the city resulted in the inevitable: abuse of power and employment of 'street' tactics by a scared, poorly trained police force."

I'm biased, but my brother is brilliant. And correct.

The Scorpion Unit that the Memphis officers worked in stands in contrast to its acronym: Street Crimes Operation to Restore Peace in Our Neighborhoods. Instead, they beat and abused people, and in Nichols' case, they killed.

Numerous reports detailed a "run tax" officers levied when someone ran. It wasn't monetary. They would beat people and then agree not to tell anyone, which apparently happened to Nichols. They had not counted on police helicopter footage.

The officers beat and kicked Nichols until he cried out for his mother, as did George Floyd.

In that case, officer Derek Chauvin knelt on Floyd's neck in a manner not unlike the way a hunter might kneel on the neck of a deer they'd shot. With the animal still alive, it's a way of hastening the death, by suffocation.

Half our population seems OK with this — and worse — when it comes to police violence victims.

It's fine, it seems, when the perp is less than human.

23/ Without Greater Transparency, Shocking Police Shootings Will Continue

January 31, 2025

Attorney LaRonna Lassiter Saunders talks to reporters during a Dec. 31, 2024, interview in Overland Park. (Sherman Smith/Kansas Reflector)

Despite video evidence showing Taylor Lowery picking up a wrench and moving away from officers before being shot dozens of times, Shawnee County District Attorney Mike Kagay continues to insist that his initial report is accurate.

This cavalier attitude — none of the agencies involved concede that the initial claims that Lowery threatened officers with a knife were untrue — seems to have permeated this case, in which Topeka police posted a clearly false statement about the October

2022 killing. This attitude suggests that police felt confident that neither the video nor the truth would ever see the light of day.

If this state does not loosen law enforcement's grip on police body camera footage, these moral and ethical outrages will only continue.

The agencies involved seem unable to admit their errors.

Said Rosie Nichols, public safety communications specialist for Topeka: "This case will be resolved in the court of law, not the court of public opinion. As such, the city will not provide further comment."

Said Melissa Underwood, communications director for the Kansas Bureau of Investigation: "Your assertion that the KBI was 'pushing a false narrative when we issued the news release' is false. In officer-involved shooting investigations, we strive to provide as much information as we can to the public as quickly as possible."

These same agencies, however, fought the release of these videos for two years.

Underwood continued: "Transparently providing preliminary details based on eyewitness statements is not, 'pushing a false narrative,' even if once the full investigation concludes, additional or differing facts become known."

If they had the videos, and fought to keep them secret, what additional facts are in the offing?

Had police been less certain the public would never see unedited footage, perhaps one of the officers would not have radioed dispatch about an aggravated assault on a law enforcement officer, when the video showed that each time police tried to confront Lowery, Lowery ran from them, not at them.

Perhaps an officer would not have told Lowery's distraught sister at the scene of the shooting that they had to shoot Lowery because he'd charged police with a knife. The footage shows the knife at the foot of one of the officers as they fired 34 shots at Lowery.

The footage also showed Lowery had picked up a wrench and was moving backward, away from police, when they began firing.

Perhaps they would not have seemingly tried to fabricate a narrative in the shooting's immediate aftermath. A detective at the scene looked into the body camera and asked if they could confirm that Lowery had a deadly weapon, to which an officer replied: "No. He had a wrench."

If they had not established that Lowery had a deadly weapon, why were they firing?

The videos also seemed to show a markedly different attitude toward a white suspect with a knife and a Black suspect with a wrench.

One video shows a then-Topeka police officer rolling up to a domestic violence scene and finding a white man walking away from the house. The man volunteered that he had a knife and a joint in his pocket. The officer asked if he could pat the man down then politely called him "bro," and let him go.

Minutes later, that same officer was firing repeatedly on a Black man holding a wrench.

No wonder they sat on this video and spent taxpayer funds to keep it hidden.

This is why Kansas so desperately needs greater transparency and access to police body camera video. Without it, law enforcement can spin any narrative with impunity. Without it, we will never permeate law enforcement's cultural membrane that keeps this behavior hidden.

One of the videos showed future Kansas Bureau of Investigation director Tony Mattivi representing one of the officers during the post-shooting interview.

This occurred shortly before Mattivi rose to his directorship, but why put someone with such deep law enforcement sympathies in charge of an organization that's supposed to hold police behavior in check?

It's a farce.

This video content suggests that law enforcement — from the officers, to the Kansas Bureau of Investigation, to the District Attorney's Office — had to have known that claims Lowery charged police with a knife were false.

But he likely has nothing to fear from this system, which treats grieving families like suspects and criminals.

"It shows the coverup from the very beginning," said attorney LaRonna Lassiter Saunders, who represents Lowery's family.

It also shows more, she said.

"Taylor Lowery didn't have to die that night," Lassiter Saunders said.

Moments before the shooting, police had nearly surrounded Lowery and were pushing him, an indication that they did not perceive him as a deadly threat. No one thought to tackle him and cuff him, or to use a Taser, she said.

Lowery's family called police that night fearing Lowery might harm himself. He'd been cutting himself — and again, whenever police confronted him, at his home and at the convenience store, he ran.

"What did he do that night to deserve the death penalty?" Lassiter Saunders said.

This lack of transparency can fuel the unchecked arrogance and bad policing in these videos. But sunlight, as we say in journalism, is the best disinfectant, and our law enforcement infrastructure seems badly infected.

Yes, arrogance.

Back in September, Lassiter Saunders told me that District Attorney Kagay "had put out a misleading report on the shooting."

Kagay told me then that he believed the report his office generated offered a thorough and accurate summary. He's still standing on this manifestly incorrect description.

"If the given quote is accurate, we believe a reckless allegation would be a more accurate way to characterize her claim," Kagay said of Lassiter Saunders last fall. "As an attorney licensed in Kansas, Ms. Saunders should be aware of the consequences of making false statements, which can lead to criminal, civil and disciplinary ramifications."

Now who should feel concerned about their license, about false statements, about criminal or civil disciplinary ramifications?

But he likely has nothing to fear from this system, which treats grieving families like suspects and criminals. Lassiter Saunders said Topeka police surreptitiously recorded her conversations with fellow lawyer Paeten Denning (the Denning Law Firm is co-counsel in the case) during their initial video viewing session.

Kagay, who produced a January 2023 report clearing the officers, seems confident that anything he's done wrong will be forgiven were he to appear before any sanctioning board, the same way Topeka police felt confident that their excesses would be forgiven by Kagay and kept out of public view.

Said Lauren Bonds, executive director of the National Police Accountability Project during an interview with *Kansas Reflector*: "I think that's how police departments, culturally, are predisposed and trained to act, in a way that defends the officers' decisions. And if there's, you know, a couple of scraps of evidence that they can put together to kind of justify the narrative of the officer, they're going to do it."

"Why would you ever give them the benefit of the doubt?" Bonds said.

We should not. We should demand even greater access and transparency to all such video evidence.

Kansas Reflector editor Sherman Smith and I posed questions to the mother of her child's slain father. Da'Mabrius Duncan talked about the emptiness of the holidays and even leaving Lowery a plate of food at the site where police killed him.

As we asked Duncan questions, Lassiter Saunders wiped away tears.

"It makes me sick to my stomach watching all of this unfold," she said.

24/ Ancient Tropes Target Black Kansas Lawmaker

April 15, 2025

Rep. Ford Carr and supporters in the gallery for his disciplinary hearing must have felt as though Kehlani and Dreamville penned the lyrics of their haunting 2023 R&B hit "Shadows," about them. The hearing unfolded with painful familiarity and hypocrisy.

Tropes, hundreds of years old. Ancient double standards. Selective outrage.

Those there supporting Carr had decades of the Black experience in the workplace under their belts and, like him, have had to walk around with their defensive dukes up. Jobs are minefields, where your ability to clothe and feed loved ones often is arbitrarily threatened.

The song opens:

I can tell
That there's something lurking in the dark
I can tell
That you're tryna catch me off guard

Carr, a Wichita Democrat, isn't the most sympathetic symbol. Video taken at a Topeka pub in January captured a stream of bile and aggression rarely heard or seen away from a street corner.

I've come to know Carr fairly well since he started at the Statehouse, and we've worked together on various projects. He's complex. He's an engineer and a martial artist. He revealed during the hearing how his father was killed.

He was accused of a broad pattern of menacing behavior, but he's not the one denying people health care. He's not the one denying children summer school meals. He's not the one hellbent on destroying public education.

Claims that he created a negative environment feel galling coming from his accusers.

Supporters love Carr's pugilistic style but worry about his defaults to coarse language and physical confrontation. They also know he's on the right side of issues and that he won't show up to a knife fight with pom poms.

Supporters also recognize the games his opponents are playing with his House seat, with his character and with his constituents. Like him, they've likely said:

> *And I'm trying my best, my best to keep*
> *from going under*
> *And it's hard to forget*
> *All the rain when we keep hearing the thunder*
> *It just feels like shadows keep following me*

Carr's supporters had a larger concern: how Black people with strong, culturally authentic voices, from Malcolm X in the 1960s to Texas Rep. Jasmine Crockett today, get policed.

There's always a color tax. Whatever problem you have in this society, if you add Black, your situation worsens. Our mistakes cost us more. Our achievements mean less.

Carr touched on this during the hearing. He said of the more than 6,000 people who have served as legislators, only 128 were Black, or 2.13%. That percentage represents more than 90 percent of legislators hauled into hearings like his.

The hearing began with an explicit show of force from Capitol police positioned in the corners of the room.

The police presence brought back a scene from the book, Just Mercy: A Story of Justice and Redemption, where police intimidated a client's supporters before a hearing with police dogs. Many remembered police unleashing dogs on peaceful civil rights protesters.

Then, a condescending warning from Committee Chairman Rep. Bob Lewis.

"This is not a political rally," Lewis said.

Lewis controlled everything from meeting times (changed multiple times without concern for Wichita constituents), meeting rooms (changed multiple times) and what evidence he would allow.

That exclusion also felt familiar. African Americans represent America's "exceptionalism" because the rights much of the country sings about while wrapping themselves in the flag, apply to everyone — *except* us.

It's why "patriots" reflexively oppose civil rights. Whenever they exalt this nation, there sit Black people bearing the scars of America's worst impulses. That's why so many eagerly want to bury evidence of those misdeeds. It is not just that they don't understand. They don't want to understand so they can luxuriate in blissful ignorance of what others must confront daily. We occupy separate realities.

Consider the presence of Republican Rep. Leah Howell, Carr's accuser.

Howell is a small white woman. She appeared in the same hearing room as the towering Carr, a Black man. Her complaint reminded me of historical dog whistles, some made famous by the racist film *Birth of a Nation.*

Rep. Henry Helgerson, the Democrat whom Carr pushed down during that bar fracas, didn't file a complaint. Howell did so instead. The same bar video showed Howell patting Carr's shoulder as tempers raged.

It would seem difficult to claim fear after doing that, but Howell did so, saying tearfully that "her conscience" compelled her to speak out, adding that she would have done the same thing had a Republican acted in similar fashion.

Only, she didn't.

In February, Republican Rep. Nick Hoheisel aggressively approached Carr, uttering profanity on the House floor. She filed no complaint.

Howell also invoked racism, which felt appropriate given that many Black Wichitans know her district for its overt racism.

During the past few decades, a cross was burned in a family's yard; residents protested the disciplining of a white child who had drawn a Confederate Battle Flag; parents hounded an educator for showing a diversity film; Black athletes have complained of crowds racially jeering at them. A mother there said bullying led her daughter to attempt suicide.

Suddenly Howell's conscience is calling? Sounds more like selective outrage.

Kansas Reflector reported in February for example, how Republican Rep. Patrick Penn joked — from the House floor — about shooting former Democratic Rep. Jason Probst in a conversation with freshman legislator Rep. Kyler Sweely, R-Hutchinson.

I guess conscience comes and goes.

Probst shared a story on his Substack blog about a racist joke told among a gaggle of Republican representatives. According to Probst, the members enjoyed the following: "What's the most confusing holiday in Ferguson, Missouri?"

Answer: "Father's Day."

For the record, a 2013 Centers for Disease Control and Prevention study found Black fathers were more involved in their children's lives than white or Hispanic fathers.

Probst added in the blog: "They (conservative leadership) actively legislate to silence any dissenting voice. They use the levers of the system they control to enforce compliance. They punish those who refuse to be controlled by the rules."

This is why they wanted to break Carr's will.

> *I felt it in my spirit. I know they try to kill it ...*
> *That two-faced shit finished.*
> *Don't push me to my limit.*

And that's the game so many people have faced at work.

> *And I'm trying my best, my best to keep*
> *from going under*
> *And it's hard to forget*
> *All the rain when we keep hearing the thunder*

I can remember a nugget of weather wisdom I received from a security guard at my first job. As we locked up and stepped out into a cloudy March night, we could hear thunder grumbling in the distance.

"That means spring is near," he said, pointing into the sky.

Maybe.

Spring symbolizes renewal and rebirth. Even resurrection for some. A new reality.

But for many of us, we only get rain.

The thunder hovers like shadows, and our springtime never arrives.

25/ The Charade Is Over

March 26, 2025

Members of the Ku Klux Klan marched on Washington, D.C., in the 1920s as the revived group flexed its political muscle. (Library of Congress)

Extremists in our Statehouse and in Washington, D.C., have busied themselves with rolling back decades of civil rights gains.

In Topeka, they quashed legally cast ballots by eliminating the three-day grace period and admitting that if they'd had their druthers, they'd eliminate all early voting.

In the nation's capital, extremists have attacked Navajo "code talkers," the Pima Indian soldier who took part of the iconic photo of American forces planting a flag on Iwo Jima, and baseball barrier-breaker Jackie Robinson.

The president's administration has lifted a ban on segregated facilities for federal contractors and has deleted more than 90 links to Congressional Medal of Honor winners of color. It feels so very bleak.

But as ugly as this seems, it also means the charade of societal equality for people of color is mercifully over. It is now clear that a majority of Americans either harbor racial biases or don't consider them serious enough to actively oppose. The question is settled. We can stop pretending. These most recent actions demonstrate that the racism they claim does not exist, really does.

These developments upend more than 50 years of denials about our racial caste system.

Back in 1968, President Johnson's Kerner Commission wrote this in a groundbreaking report: "White society is deeply implicated in the ghetto. White institutions created it, white institutions maintain it, and white society condones it."

A carefully orchestrated counter-campaign of deny, delay and deflect followed.

We caught glimpses of it in Lee Atwater's infamous 1981 interview about Nixon's "Southern Strategy," the plan by which Presidents Nixon and Regan converted Dixie Democrats.

"You start out in 1954 by saying, 'N*****, n*****, n*****. By 1968 you can't say 'n*****' — that hurts you, backfires. So, you say stuff like, uh, forced busing, states' rights, and all that stuff, and you're getting so abstract. Now, you're talking about cutting taxes, and all these things you're talking about are totally economic things and a byproduct of them is, Blacks get hurt worse than whites. ... 'We want to cut this,' is much more abstract than even the busing thing, uh, and a hell of a lot more abstract than 'N*****N, n*****.'"

A common strategy from these extremists is attacking their opponent's greatest strength, and in this case, it's the hundreds of years of history demonstrating that the nation's founders used race as one of its organizing principles. It is a tacit admission of what that side fears most — truth.

This remains manifestly true, but the current administration continues the ruse.

"We have ended the tyranny of so-called diversity, equity and inclusion policies all across the entire federal government and, indeed, the private sector and our military," the president said during his recent speech to the joint session of Congress. "And our country will be woke no longer."

So, the *victims* of hundreds of years of tyranny are the tyrants?

Black median household wealth stood at $24,100 in 2019. White median household wealth stood at $188,200. Black unemployment has remained roughly twice that of the white unemployment and as expected, Black people remain disproportionately impoverished.

Diversity policies represent mere remedies for historic inequality. Ending them assumes the society has achieved social equality. This is ending the remedy without addressing the central issue of inequality. It leaves the unfair system untouched, so that those who've always had an advantage maintain their edge, and punishes those already behind.

How can 60 years of half-hearted equality efforts address 335 years of enslavement and segregation? They can't. That span lasted from 1619 to 1954.

Racists killed Emmett Till the following year. The Montgomery Bus Boycott also began in 1955.

This is like debating climate change. We know it exists, but powerful voices need it not to, so this odd dance around the truth continues.

Wrote Ta-Nehisi Coates in his latest book, *The Message*, "Some people's credits earned them more, and their mistakes cost them less. And those people who took more and paid less lived in a world of iniquitous wealth, while his own people lived in a world of terrifying want."

A cruel pettiness remains a part of this dance.

In the past, towns passed laws saying Black people couldn't play chess or checkers with white people or that Black drivers couldn't pass white drivers in traffic or use the same pay phones. Today, it is Defense Secretary Pete Hegseth threatening to drum Black people out of the military because of razor bumps or pseudofoliculitis.

The Rev. Martin Luther King Jr. came to this sad realization near the end of his life after years of fighting for equality. King said he'd taken many white people at their word that they wanted to end discrimination.

"White America is not even psychologically organized to close the gap," King said in his last book, *Where Do We Go from Here: Chaos or Community?* "Essentially, it seeks only to make it less painful, less obvious, but in most respects, to maintain it."

When I led the Kansas African American Museum, we received the donation of a Ku Klux Klan robe and mask (more than once), found by family members of a deceased patriarch. The family would not fill out

This is like debating climate change. We know it exists, but powerful voices need it not to, so this odd dance around the truth continues.

the provenance documents. They didn't want any lasting connection to their horrifying finds.

We eventually put the robes on a mannequin for an exhibition on racial terror. A guest, there for other business, left shaken by the display. I decided to never put it out again.

The guest said that as a boy in Mississippi, his father left him in the car to run a quick errand as Klansmen gathered nearby. His father gave him a haunting command.

"Don't look them in the eye."

By staring too long, they may think you know them and then, they start reaching for torches and rifles.

This represented the real power of the so-called "invisible empire." With faces hidden, people never knew if the judge, or the policeman, or their doctor held membership in the Klan. This is how racism has operated, under sheets of denial.

But now that the pretense that racism doesn't exist has dropped, we absolutely must look these people and practices in the eye. The nation has an opportunity to vomit up all the bilious myths and stereotypes that continue to threaten our stability as a nation.

We no longer have to pretend. This is no longer a theory. It's out in the open now. We don't have to hide.

And there's an incredible blessing in all of this — if we face it.

26/ Are We Decent Enough to Let Others Merge?

March 12, 2024

Think of our society as a vast human highway guiding people toward opportunity.

Most of us occupy the slow lane on the right. A dwindling number occupy the safe, middle lane. A privileged few zoom to opportunity in the fast lane. But a minority group had no on-ramp to that road. So, we created on-ramps.

That's really all affirmative action is. An on-ramp to opportunity.

But now, you can hear the shrieks of terror from the fast lane about how there isn't enough room on the human highway. If these people aren't on the highway, they must not be qualified. They thunder about what on-ramps might cost while ignoring their own frivolous spending.

But, as the Eagles sang, that's "life in the fast lane. Surely make you lose your mind."

In late January, Rep. Steven Howe, R-Salina, chairman of the House Higher Education Budget Committee, argued that diversity, equity, and inclusion efforts at colleges and universities needed guardrails.

"What we've seen across the United States is universities becoming more lopsided in terms of the types of people that are in positions," Howe said in a *Kansas Reflector* article. "They might be more politically minded in a certain viewpoint. You

It isn't about getting the job as much as landing in the interview pool.

might not have a diversity of intellectual thought on a campus because you've kind of weeded out people that may not share in a certain ideology."

I wonder how many campuses he visited and if Kansas taxpayers were on the hook for those trips.

They've been working on this for a couple of sessions now. Last year, extremists sought to prohibit state universities from questioning faculty, students, and contractors about diversity, equity and inclusion.

"House Bill 2460 would prohibit public colleges and universities from including DEI as a provision for admission, financial aid, or employment decisions," according to the Kansas Reflector article. "These decisions could not factor in candidates' support or opposition to 'any political ideology or movement, including a pledge or statement regarding diversity, equity, inclusion, patriotism or related topics.'"

As "proof," Howe reportedly showed his committee a university job application for an assistant professor position, which required a statement of diversity, equity, and inclusion, saying such requirements tended to "discriminate against people who might not adhere to their orthodoxy."

Orthodoxy? You mean, like democracy?

We want to hire people at public universities who are hostile to the idea of equity and fairness?

These folks are in deep denial, and as J. Peterman of *Seinfeld* fame said: "The toll road of denial is a long and dangerous one. The price? Your soul."

These measures are about protecting advantages gained over decades and centuries. The current system advantages people at the middle of our caste system and up. Many of these folks oppose fairness policies because they really need the advantage.

Some need the head start or they can't compete.

But no one is guaranteed success.

Once on the highway, people still have to merge. They still have to make their own progress. It isn't about getting the job as much as it is about just landing in the interview pool. Having access to advantages that people have been denied for decades.

People think of this as a Black issue, but it isn't.

"There is no Negro problem," said Frederick Douglass more than a century ago. "The problem is whether the American people have the loyalty enough, honor enough, patriotism enough, to live up to their own Constitution."

In this case, the question remains: Are we decent enough to just let somebody merge? And please bear in mind, we aren't even thinking about the people living under the highway.

But while occupying the *poll* position, the folks in the fast lane want a wider lane for themselves and fewer on-ramps for you.

27/ Black Republicans Enjoy Limited Support

June 11, 2023

Black Republican Rep. Patrick Penn accused Gov. Laura Kelly of advancing bigoted expectations recently, after she used her line-item veto to roll back $250,000 in funding aimed at historic Quindaro. Abolitionists founded the settlement along the Underground Railroad to help the enslaved flee bondage in Missouri in the 1850s.

"Diversity of thought exists in the Black community just like every other," Penn said in an interview with Fox News. "No other race has the expectation placed upon them by white liberal elites that we line up and vote for Democrats like the Black community does. Such bigoted expectations are both unfortunate relics of a small-minded past and simply unconscionable."

That's bold talk for someone seemingly so out of step with Black political sensibilities. Penn and Black Republicans increasingly claim to speak for the Black collective, but they shouldn't. They represent a political party that too often seems hostile to issues African Americans support. As we approach Juneteenth and commemorate a centuries-long quest for freedom, this distinction remains important.

Of the 26 majority Black congressional districts nationally, not one has elected a Republican. That's less about lockstep loyalty and more about the Republican Party standing out of alignment with Black political beliefs. Black voters, like any segment of the population, vote their interests, and

Black conservatives are viewed as proxies for white, conservative interests.

A Pew Research Center poll found that Black Republicans are less likely than Black Democrats to have strong ties to Black identity or other Black people, and are less likely to attend a Black church.

Not all Black Republicans function this way, but many do.

For example, Penn lobbied freshman Rep. Marvin Robinson, elected by a deep-blue constituency, to vote with Republicans nearly 70% of the time. Robinson voted with Republicans against food stamps, against Medicaid expansion and for a measure that would complicate vote counting. Robinson and Penn's votes don't represent the beliefs of most Black voters.

Don't forget Daniel Cameron, the Kentucky attorney general now running for governor, who refused to charge the Louisville police officers who killed Breonna Taylor in her bed. Or Herschel Walker, the failed and confused Georgia senatorial candidate very few African Americans supported. Or South Carolina senator and presidential candidate Tim Scott, who denies the existence of structural racism.

Penn was right, there is diversity of Black thought. But his rhetoric is misleading. Maybe even intentionally.

I reached out to him via email but didn't hear back. I was curious about his connections to the Black community. Was he raised in one? Does he volunteer in these communities? How has he developed sensibilities about the Black experience? I'd still welcome that conversation.

Attacking Kelly, Penn said in the Fox interview: "Democrats owned Marvin's great, great grandfather down in Texas, so it's no small idea that they think

For decades, many Black voters, like my great-grandfather, voted with Republicans because President Abraham Lincoln and the GOP ended Slavery.

that they own his vote in the Kansas Legislature, as well."

Penn is either disingenuous or uninformed about how race realigned American party politics in the 1960s. For decades, many Black voters, like my great-grandfather, voted with Republicans because President Abraham Lincoln and the GOP ended slavery, but the parties flipped in 1964. Historian and Atlanta native Taylor Branch discussed this with his hometown newspaper, the Atlanta Journal-Constitution, in a 2013 interview.

"Most Americans need to be reminded that race and race alone had the power to turn our partisan politics upside down in one year — 1964," Branch told the newspaper. "Before 1964, you could not win elected office in the South if you proposed any change to segregation."

Branch said as the Senate prepared to vote on the Civil Rights Act, then U.S.-Sen. Barry Goldwater announced he would vote against it and received a 75-page legal opinion from William Rehnquist and Robert Bork on why politicians should oppose the Civil Rights Act.

"That moment was the catalyst that changed American politics to this day, because as soon as he said, 'I'm going to vote against the Civil Rights Bill,' you had candidates across the South springing up and saying, 'I'm going to be a Republican,'" Branch said.

In a summer, Branch said, the parties realigned over President Lyndon Johnson's federal attack on segregation.

Goldwater, Rehnquist and Bork "made resentment of the federal government respectable," Branch said. "That kind of resentment, the notion that government is bad, grew out of resentment of the Civil Rights Act, and it has lasted ever since."

Black Republicans parrot the same "small government, state's rights" arguments, clearly out of touch with Black voters today and historically. In his most famous speech, Martin Luther King Jr. referenced Alabama's governor as "having his lips dripping with the words of interposition and nullification," a direct reference to Southern efforts to keep the federal government from rescuing terrorized Black citizens.

White Republican politicians in the South used the fear of racial progress — the Southern Strategy — to lure white voters to a new GOP.

Even today, the GOP maintains an anti-civil rights posture. As protests against police terror crested in 2020 for example, conservatives smeared protesters as "woke." When the House of Representatives voted overwhelmingly to make Juneteenth a federal holiday, 14 House members — all Republicans — voted against it.

Should Black voters distrust Democrats, too? Certainly. Black voters are often forgotten until election time. Many people have legitimately questioned African Americans' strong yet unrequited devotion to the Democratic party. Over the years, for professional reasons, I've registered as a Republican, as a Democrat and as an independent.

But Black voters do understand who makes it difficult for them to vote. We do know who supports the largely white and conservative police unions and who refuse to even discuss qualified immunity. We do know who racially gerrymandered Wyandotte County, Robinson's district.

Look, Penn persuaded Robinson to abandon his constituents and colleagues, and all's fair in love and politics. But Penn doesn't get to throw down race cards like he's playing spades.

Democrats may once have owned Robinson's grandfather.

But if Robinson's grandfather were around today and needed help, it would be Penn and his pals — not white, liberal Democrats — who last session would have ensured that Robinson's grandfather couldn't eat, couldn't access health insurance, and couldn't vote.

Such policy positions are unfortunate relics of a small-minded past and simply unconscionable.

28/ Don't Understand Trump Supporters? Remember Bill Clinton Supporters?

August 3, 2024

Republican presidential nominee and former President Donald Trump is questioned by journalists at the National Association of Black Journalists convention in Chicago on Wednesday, July 31, 2024. The event was moderated by, from left, Rachel Scott, senior congressional correspondent for ABC News; Kadia Goba, politics reporter at Semafor; and Harris Faulkner, anchor of* The Faulkner Focus *and co-host of Outnumbered on Fox News. (William J. Ford/Maryland Matters)

Former President Donald Trump told multiple lies minutes into his appearance onstage at the National Association of Black Journalists annual convention in Chicago this week.

He said ABC News' Rachel Scott launched into "horrible" and "nasty" questions without greeting him. Scott had just shaken his hand as he walked on stage and thanked him for his time.

He would claim to not know what DEI stood for despite his party targeting diversity, equity and inclusion efforts nationally, including here in Kansas. He falsely claimed that liberals favored executing babies in the ninth month and even after birth.

Trump speaks with the precision of a rusty butcher knife. He's constantly and obviously lying, understanding that so-called real-time fact checking could not keep pace with his gushing, fire hydrant stream of untruths. How could anyone support him?

It's now the left's turn to deal with a political opponent they can't believe anyone supports, kind of like how conservatives must have felt dealing with former President Bill Clinton. The parallels boggle the mind.

Let's start with the lies.

Clinton famously claimed to not have inhaled when first trying marijuana. When pressed about his affair with a White House intern, he said in a dodge, "it depends on what your definition of 'is' is." He said he didn't have sexual relations with "that woman."

Both seem to have mastered not just the blood sport of politics, but they also have a penchant for frustrating and confounding their political opponents with how little crime or controversy sticks to their Teflon brands.

Clinton and Trump each have sycophantic supporters.

African Americans literally referred to Clinton as the first Black president and cheered him loudly during a late-night talk show appearance when he donned Wayfarers and played saxophone.

Trump supporters, many of whom are evangelical Christians, have created an almost Messianic aura around Trump, who famously said he could shoot someone on Fifth Avenue in New York and his supporters wouldn't care.

Their opponents hate them and their respective political bases worship them for it.

Clinton and Trump both seem to have little regard for women and the word "no." Both made jaunts to Jeffery Epstein's island of child sex trafficking, and both have faced numerous and credible accusations from women about their behavior.

Both dodged the draft and Vietnam.

Character remained an important trait until Clinton.

Today, Trump benefits from that shift in political mores.

Both enriched themselves in office. Clinton sold nights in the Lincoln bedroom and reached out to China for donations. Trump steered people wanting an audience with him to his gold-ticket hotel nearby, where the U.S. Secret Service also had to pay for their rooms.

Clinton and Trump floated policies that hurt their rock-solid bases of support.

Prison building exploded under Clinton and helped create the current mass incarceration crisis that has made America the world's most punitive nation, with two million people locked up. That's roughly 25% of the world's prison population.

Trump delayed court proceedings on the Obama administration's expansion of overtime. He tried to cut his own taxes while wresting health insurance away from tens of millions of Americans. He proposed budget cuts that would devastate rural America.

Everyone feels sorry for both of their wives.

There are differences for sure.

First and foremost, Clinton didn't help organize a riot at the Capitol. Trump did.

Clinton was a Rhodes and Fulbright Scholar. Trump attended college. Clinton, for all his lustful meandering, seemed to care for the poor and working classes. Trump says he loves the uneducated, but probably only because that makes them easier to manipulate.

Clinton was a statesman. A long-winded statesman, but a statesman. Trump likes dictators.

We're living in historic times. Never has a Black woman stood so close to the American presidency, and never has a wide swath of us stood so close to civil war in modern times. The country teeters at a demographic tipping point.

About half the nation saw Trump's NABJ visit for what it was: a not-so-veiled attempt to sow racial distrust of Vice President Kamala Harris among Black voters, an effort to pit the Black working class and poor against immigrants, and to show his base he ain't afraid of negroes.

Trump would disrespect those uppity Negroes right to their face at one of their most revered organizations. Kind of like Clinton did to Jesse Jackson, when Clinton bashed hip-hop artist and activist Sistah Souljah at a Jackson-sponsored event.

I can't for the life of me understand how anyone could respect Trump. But I do remember liking Clinton, so yes, I guess I resemble today's Trumper.

I can't for the life of me understand how anyone could respect Trump. But I do remember liking Clinton, so yes, I guess I resemble today's Trumper.

What's beyond belief, it increasingly seems, is a
different point of view.

151

Note: Toni Morrison calling Clinton the first Black
president referred to his poor background and the
persecution he experienced according to T'Nahesi Coates
in the *Atlantic,* August 15, 2015.

29/ The Abuse of Black Student Athletes

December 15, 2022

Toni Morrison's The Bluest Eye *was among more than two dozen books removed from a school library at Goddard following a challenge by a parent. The books have since been returned to the shelves. (Max McCoy/ Kansas Reflector)*

When I heard my son's voice for the first time as he entered the world, his cry punched right through me. I gave him his first bath and shampoo. I fed him first. I held him in my lap and stared down at him for hours.

I was there when he lost his first tooth, when he skinned his knee the first time and for his first play in Wichita Children's Theater. As I wrote my first book, he slept beside me on the couch as I pounded a laptop, stopping to feed and change him when he woke up. I tried to attend his performances.

I didn't make all of them, including some in rural areas where it seems more common for audiences to racially target Black student athletes from the stands. Recent news reports termed descriptions of what happened during a Valley Center basketball game "exaggerated" or "overblown."

Well, exaggerated and overblown didn't stop some legislators from falsely claiming critical race theory dominated school curriculums. It hasn't stopped parents and others from protesting books about Black lives in school libraries. If people believed in the deep harm from learning history or even reading about Black people's experiences, where's the commensurate concern about Black student safety?

State education officials need to step in here with the same urgency of the CRT make-believe scare and library challenges for this actual danger. Facing mobs can prove terrifying and traumatizing for Black students.

I'm chairman of the Kansas African American Affairs Commission. Fellow commissioner Jonathan McRoy, who represents Wichita, reached out to me about the Valley Center incident. I told McRoy that Valley Center wasn't alone.

My cousin who works with Wyandotte High students, for example, said students witnessed similar behavior in Augusta. A former colleague said she'd experienced racist taunts in Derby. Hispanic students elsewhere have heard "Build That Wall!"

My son, now a college student, said he'd experienced this.

When he traveled to Chaparral High School for a football game in which he was the only Black child on his team, he said that crowd waved Confederate battle flags and Trump flags. He was sent on an errand, alone, into that crowd.

Some of his Independent School classmates, he said, called him the "N-word." Others called his mother "Chewbacca," the bellowing, ape-like creature from the Star Wars franchise. One of his white teammates literally spat on a Black teammate — and remained on the team.

When he played for Olathe East and his football team traveled to Gardner, he said people targeted Black players with ape sounds. He didn't share these incidents immediately. They seeped from his memory as his struggles mounted.

I'd tried preparing my sons for racist behavior. I shared books like *The Autobiography of Malcolm X* and *Before the Mayflower* that talked about the challenges faced by Black people. But along the way I wondered if I were stealing their innocence.

My son, however, called this intervention "life saving."

Author Stephen King once described isolation as horror's key ingredient. That was what my son said he felt. He described not just Chaparral but also private school life as, at times, horrifying.

He said he struggled to maintain his cultural identity but watched some Black students assimilate to the point where they'd amputated any racial semblance of themselves. He described this absorption as a kind of death.

"What I picked up most when you were teaching me about Black history was if you don't know where

I'd tried preparing my sons for racist behavior. I wondered if I were stealing their innocence. My son, however, called this intervention "life saving."

you came from, especially as a Black man, a part of you, dies.

"I never wanted to be the person who died."

There were echoes of Toni Morrison's *The Bluest Eye* that my son successfully navigated — he understood his intrinsic human value, whether or not his skin was white and whether or not his eyes were blue.

Many Black children become adults who succumb to toxic, racial beauty standards.

This trauma is what we force on students by not stopping this behavior. It comes from not sharing the perspectives of others through literature and other means.

My adult niece, who now has a child of her own, used to perform with a Valley Center High School dance team.

"I can assure you, this is a normal thing that the student section does during basketball games!" she said. "I HATED having to stand with the student section hearing things they would shout and say about Black players."

A high school classmate who attended Valley Center elementary and junior high schools said, "it was very difficult dealing with the very open racism that was carried out by the students and staff — yes, even some of the teachers."

Another high school classmate, however, said she'd attended games and insisted the behavior in question "was not racial."

So why did the Valley Center School District apologize?

"They did have a reason to apologize," she wrote. "There was an inappropriate yell at someone shooting a free throw. That was addressed quickly. But there is no evidence of all the other stuff they say happened."

She added: "The Topeka crowd was harassing VC crowd after the game. But (news media) did not mention any of that, did they?"

Interesting how it was the mob that was threatened in her view.

A news website blurred crowd photos taken at the reputed Valley Center basketball game. The blurring of the photos seemed sadly on brand. The privacy of people accused of bad behavior seemed more important than the actual safety of Black youth subjected to ugly, public behavior.

I propose that superintendents and school boards watch this issue closely, so the next time Black student athletes experience this, they're not facing the hecklers alone, but with the full-throated support of the moral majority behind them.

If nothing else, we owe them protection.

30/ All-White Panel Refused Black Kansas Student's Transfer

February 5, 2023

The Kansas State High School Athletic Association denied Zion Young's transfer request from Campus High School. (Steve Young)

The recent 4-2 denial of Zion Young's transfer request by an all-white KSHSAA board represents an exploitative American sporting system.

If this story consisted only of the Kansas State High School Athletic Association's denial of Zion Young's transfer request from Campus High School following a documented and undisputed racist incident, it would still document a sizeable concern that too would amount to a sizeable problem.

But what happened to Zion — and has happened to too many talented and Black athletes — feels bigger. That recent 4-2 denial vote before an all-white KSHSAA board represented an American sporting system that exploits Black bodies. These systems should elevate, celebrate, and liberate Black athletes.

Was Zion's request denied because the requested transfer would have been his third in four years? Was it because his father, Steve Young, is an influential

AAU coach resented because of his past recruitment of prep stars Buddy Hield and Perry Ellis? Was it systemic racism?

Whatever the answer, we can't leave kids vulnerable to the racism Zion encountered, to potential petty jealousies or unfair restrictions on chasing dreams.

Steve Young said his son was a victim of a racist act, then a racially insensitive review system that minimized what his son experienced.

"My whole point is to expose these people," Steve Young said.

I asked KSHSAA executive director Bill Faflick for his organization's side of the story, along with the number of transfer request denials and a racial breakdown of the requests and denials. The public has a right to know if data show that transfer rulings unfairly target Black athletes.

Faflick said KSHSAA does not discuss the specifics of a student transfer beyond family and educator stakeholders, but he said there were no data supporting claims the transfer process disproportionately disadvantages Black athletes.

"The appeal board listened to appellants (sic) perspective as well as the former school administrator and staff regarding the transfer, and ultimately the Appeal Board did not believe this warranted a hardship," Faflick said in an emailed response.

Faflick said once the association receives paperwork, it cannot discern the race of the transferring student. I pointed out that not collecting racial data doesn't mean a problem doesn't exist. He added that the organization "strives to apply the rules equally regardless of student gender, race, activity, school or any other factor."

He said KSHSAA approves most transfers. For foreign exchange students, 294 of 296. For hardship-transfer applications, 173 of 206. All of the 302 limited eligibility applications were approved.

Faflick confirmed that Zion faced an all-white panel but said that the organization had African Americans on its executive board and board of directors. (It appears, however, that only two of 65 top administrators are Black.) He said rules governing transfers are there to protect students from displacement in activities by students engaged in "school shopping."

He said to transfer, a student must meet all other "rules and regulations, such as age, Scholarship, Bona Fide Student in Good Standing, etc."

Finally, Faflick said KSHSAA does not control membership of the Appeal Board as it is elected by those in the respective category from those willing to serve.

But Black students, at least in urban districts, are overrepresented in basketball and football. Zion shouldn't have had to face an all-white panel to escape the racism at his high school. A more representative board might have better understood Zion's plight.

Those regulations feel archaic in today's bold new world of sports entertainment.

Schools and advertisers court top-tier Black athletes. For greater athletic success, for career advancement, and for profits including new opportunities with name, image and likeness deals, these athletes begin weighing earlier than ever where to find the best deals and exposure as well as safe spaces to pursue their dreams. Individual athletes are now essentially small businesses.

Steve Young said his son was a victim of a racist act, then a racially insensitive review system that minimized what his son experienced.

And while student athletes now use the college transfer portal liberally, this newfound freedom has begun to irk some traditionalists.

It's different for white athletes, who tend to have the means and connections to navigate these outdated systems. This opportunity imbalance disproportionately stymies Black upward mobility.

Steve Young rejected KSHSAA accusations that Zion was "school shopping."

"We were happy at the school for two years until the racist incident," Steve Young said in a call. "We didn't go looking until this racial incident occurred. If this isn't a hardship, then what is?"

The school denied the transfer request and so did KSHSAA, meaning Zion lost the opportunity to play basketball while finishing his high school career.

That "incident" involved a PowerPoint presentation depicting Zion as a gorilla with enormous lips.

"No one cared about my son's well-being," said Steve Young, who has since moved his son to a private, Christian Wichita school. "They're just mad because they wanted my son to play for them."

Zion slipped into depression, even breaking out in hives. His grades slumped. He'd become truant.

The family wanted Zion, whose parents are divorced, to move in with his mother, Tina, a principal in the Wichita School District. She lived in the Wichita Heights attendance zone, but the KSHSAA hearing didn't go well, Steve Young said. They weren't allowed to cross-examine anyone during the hearing.

"My son was discriminated against twice — once at the school and again in front of that board," Steve Young said. "The system failed him."

Unfairness seems endemic.

Jalen Rose, an ESPN talk show host who founded and runs a Detroit-based charter school, said restrictions on young Black athletes aren't new. For example, he said, basketball and football leagues restrict professional participation immediately after high school and limit contract lengths.

"In baseball, you can sign a 10-year deal," Rose said. "In hockey, you can sign a nine-year deal. You can't in basketball. In tennis, golf, and NASCAR, you can turn pro after high school. You can't in basketball and football. … They are going to force you to feed these systems as long as possible."

Sometimes, it's just old-fashioned racism in the youth sports world.

Black athletes playing basketball or football in Wichita during the 1960s said white coaches told them that while they were good enough to play or to even start, only a few were allowed on any one team. This denied many of them college athletic scholarships.

The unfair treatment didn't end in the 1960s.

Co-writing Barry Sanders' 2003 bestselling book, I learned that few Big 8 conference football recruiters asked about him because they were told our school had no major college talent. There were whispers that Barry's frenetic running style meant he lacked contact courage. This limited his options.

Sanders later won the Heisman and the National Football League's Rookie of the Year. He was voted into the Hall of Fame. He obviously persisted, but no person or group should be able to narrow a kid's horizon this way.

"No one cared about my son's well-being... they're just mad because they wanted my son to play for them."

They shouldn't be able to limit Zion's life and future the way KSHAAA did.

The sad truth is, Black people don't enjoy dominion over our bodies. We learned from events in Memphis we don't have that dominion in traffic stops. We learned from Trayvon Martin that we don't have that dominion walking home from a store. We learned from Ahmaud Arbury that we don't have that dominion while jogging. We learned from Breanna Taylor that we don't have that dominion while we sleep.

We certainly don't have it in sports.

So what do we know?

We know Zion did not ask classmates to depict him as an ape. His father said the family received no apologies and when Zion wanted to transfer, a ruling body of white adults minimized what happened, then denied his transfer, ultimately demanding he remain in a toxic environment if he wanted to play basketball.

We must weed out gatekeepers wielding capricious power over Black athletes.

"They knew what happened to him, and they knew basketball was what he loved, and then they took it from him," Steve Young said. "We don't want this to happen to another kid."

We must weed out gatekeepers wielding capricious power over Black athletes.

31/ Persistent Denial

June 18, 2024

Few images from the violent attacks on peacefully demonstrating teens from civil rights-era demonstrations convey the brutality of the era more than scenes from 1963 Birmingham and the powerful blasts from fire hoses and water cannons.

Pressure from the hoses and water cannons — as much as 100 PSI — could break ribs. Rip out hair. Segregationists pummeled the youths marching for voting rights the way a gardener might scatter fresh-cut grass with a leaf blower.

To the men behind those hoses and cannons, the youths and other Black people counted as little more than yard clippings because white Southerners as children fed on a "lost cause" narrative allowing them to think of their activities as something noble or patriotic. The adults beating well-dressed teenagers at lunch counter sit-ins, the women haranguing the Little Rock Nine as they entered school and others sitting in White Citizen Council meetings were taught about the lost cause.

They acted according to those teachings.

Current efforts on the right to erase or dilute our racial history should frighten us. Attempting to erase the past, alter textbooks and misremember history, we are creating new generations of people committed to our centuries-old racial caste system.

People hopeful about achieving racial healing once reassured themselves that when the older generation died, the nation could move on. But people who know better have prepared more stale, racist bread for new generations to consume.

This looks like history on repeat.

Historian Richard Slotkin writes about this in his book, *A Great Disorder: National Myth and the Battle for America.*

"MAGA's use of myth gives its adherents the sense of righteous empowerment that comes from association with a deeply rooted historical tradition," Slotkin writes. "But its embrace of Lost Cause symbolism carries with it a commitment to the myth's political action script of cultural and political authoritarianism. Thus, MAGA has become a distinctly American approach to fascism: more neo-Confederate than neo-Nazi, an amalgam of American exceptionalism, racial and ethnic bigotry, Christian nationalism, and neoliberal economics."

The irony here is that this long, unbroken resistance to fairness made diversity, equity and inclusion programs — efforts those on the right call racist — urgently necessary.

As Grace Paley, a teacher and poet and activist once said: "We are in the hands of men whose power and wealth have separated them from the reality of daily life and from the imagination. We are right to be afraid."

Historians have said for years that the Confederacy lost the war but won the narrative.

Journalist and historian Jon Meacham talked about Edward Alfred Pollard authoring the post-Civil War "lost cause" narrative, a story that has endured all these decades later.

"Because the war itself was lost, the war over slavery had been lost, that the South should not reengage in a force of arms," Meacham said in a speech shown on C-SPAN. "But it should reengage in a battle of ideas where the enemy was declared to be the forces of centralization centered in Washington.

"It was an animating narrative that urged those who harbored a deep belief in white supremacy to give them hope, to continue to fight."

That narrative continues to animate.

Just last month, a Virginia school board voted to restore the names of two schools to Confederate generals who led the pro-slavery South during the Civil War. Right-wing US textbooks describe the horrors of slavery as "Black immigration," and the enslaved as "workers." One Black Florida politician seemed to suggest recently that segregation promoted positive outcomes for Black families.

In this narrative, there's also a tacit admission that the history under attack is so potent that it must never be seen or heard or read widely. This is why detractors don't want it discussed. Any cursory exploration would demand immediate redress.

This lost cause narrative still seems to resonate.

It's powerful enough to convince otherwise sentient beings that it's OK to run over peaceful protesters. That Kyle Rittenhouse did nothing wrong. That the Confederacy wasn't racist. That the Jan. 6, 2021, rioters who defecated in the Capital are political prisoners. On this 60th anniversary of Freedom Summer, it seems that everything old is new again.

Renewed calls for "law and order" in a country with two million people in prison. Voter suppression meant to maintain power. Attacking diversity and equality. Banning books about the Black experience.

The history under attack is so potent that it must never be seen or heard or read widely. This is why detractors don't want it discussed. any cursory exploration would demand immediate redress.

But we can't forget about those brave youths who faced those bludgeoning hoses and water cannons.

These are ominous times, especially when we consider this line from the old spiritual: "God gave Noah the rainbow sign, no more water, but the fire next time."

32/ Was Dr. King "Woke"?

April 16, 2023

Kansas legislative leaders have shrieked for weeks about a supposed wild-left "woke" agenda, promising an alternate agenda moored in the protection of mores that remain perfectly safe. They use phrases like "sexualized, woke agenda," and "radicalized woke agenda."

The term "woke," as used by Kansas legislators, seems to serve as shorthand for liberation efforts running counter to white, Christian, conservative narratives.

But this begs the question: How would yesterday's heroes fare under the woke lens of vague outrage? For instance, was civil rights icon Diane Nash woke? The Rev. Martin Luther King Jr.? Oliver Brown? Measure their sacrificial greatness against current anti-reform rantings, and we see this woke narrative for the hollow trope it is.

Chase Billingham, associate professor of sociology at Wichita State University, said the broad application of "wokeness" is no accident.

"It means everything and nothing," Billingham said. "Very much like (what's been done to) critical race theory. There are real life-and-death issues at stake in politics today, and making the fights about language and terminology distracts from discussions of real policies that have material impacts on the lives of working people."

It's a familiar play: Divide, distort and distract, but this flimsy narrative melts under history's heat.

Sixty years ago this year, segregationists murdered four little girls at Birmingham's 16th Street Baptist Church. The bombing nearly derailed Nash's nonviolent voting rights work. I asked her about this years ago when she visited Kansas.

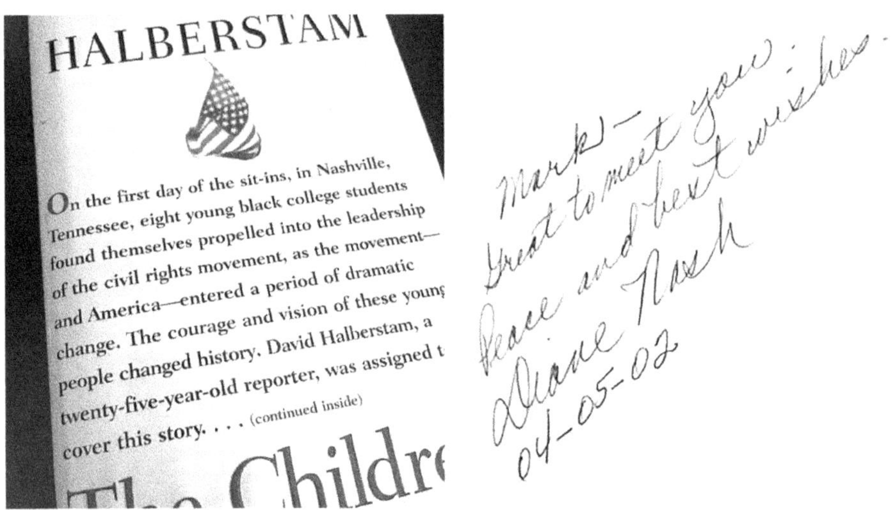

"In preparation for my interview with iconic civil rights activist Diane Nash, I purchased and read The Children ***by the great David Halberstam. When I met Nash in person, she graciously signed my copy." (Mark McCormick)***

Nash, a 1960s student at Nashville's Fisk University, said while externally composed, terror thrashed in her gut. She worried someone following her might die. She worried she might die.

"I was always so scared," said Nash, who participated in the perilous Freedom Rides through Alabama and Mississippi, while pregnant.

They expected violence, she said, but at first felt the girls' murder couldn't go unanswered. Children had to remain off limits.

"We wouldn't be able to respect ourselves," she thought then. "One of the things we considered was making sure that whoever did it, died."

They ultimately rejected violence, reasoning people could protect their children through the right to vote. They promised God and each other they would make that happen. Barely into their 20s, they signed their will, boarded buses, and bravely drove into crowds of baseball bats, fiery hatred, and flying fists.

John Seigenthaler, the former journalist and assistant to the assistant attorney general in the Kennedy administration, begged Nash to abandon the Freedom Rides. Seigenthaler, whom I'd met as a college journalist when he was American Society of Newspaper Editors board president, understood the dangers.

Southern police conspired with segregationists who burned the buses and attacked the college kids as they stumbled out gasping.

But for her transformational bravery, for her work narrowing the gap between who America claimed to be and what it was, for seeking voting rights for Black Southerners, Nash would be considered "woke" today.

So would civil rights lawyer Don Hollowell, the Kansas native who defended Black clients in front of all-white juries in violently segregated Georgia and once helped free King from prison following a traffic infraction.

So would the Rev. James Reeb, the white, Unitarian minister and Kansas native killed marching for Black voting rights in Alabama. But for Reeb's martyrdom, we might not have the Voting Rights Act.

So would Rosa Parks, the mother of the civil rights movement and so would King, who led the Montgomery bus boycott Parks launched.

So would Bayard Rustin, a lead organizer of the March on Washington, which turns 60 this year.

So would Topekan Rev. Oliver Brown, who believed his daughter shouldn't have to walk past a school in her neighborhood to attend a segregated school far away.

These examples unmask the woke narrative as a manufactured grievance, derisive shorthand for people inordinately concerned about attacks on civil rights and others who still believe voting is a right and that Democracy is sacred.

Tiny seeds of truth float in some of the claims from the right, but those isolated seeds have been greenhoused into a ginned up crisis, similarly to how Professor Harold Hill convinced River City that the presence of a new pool table threatened that town's morality.

People conscious of systemic injustice used to call themselves "conscious." Today, consciousness earns practitioners badges of shame.

In the 1984 thriller *The Terminator,*" when "Skynet" became "self-aware," it became an existential threat. In the 1999 sci-fi classic *The Matrix*, the story hinged on people ingesting pills enabling them to surface from semi-consciousness to see how machines had transformed them into batteries powering their own captivity.

So consciousness, whether dystopian or in 2023's Kansas Legislature, makes you dangerous, particularly when the point seems to divide, distract and distort. Discouraging consciousness enables the weakening of our democracy, bill by agonizing bill. Kleptocracy requires a slumbering public.

Mark Twain once said, "Sometimes I wonder whether the world is being run by smart people who are putting us on, or by imbeciles who really mean it."

He got it mostly right, but these are smart people who know precisely what they're doing.

33/ Disingenuous Demand for "Extreme Safety" in Elections

October 16, 2022

Despite the safety all around us, writes Mark McCormick, we are harmfully preoccupied with crime and threats.

Political pundits say some November election candidates will once again try to make crime a campaign issue. Crime unfailingly fires up some voters, despite the fact that the people most obsessed with it are probably the safest people on earth.

The United States represents 5% of the world's population but houses 25% of the world's prisoners. It's a stunning irony. The safest people seem preoccupied to the point of neurosis with safety and comfort. If locking people up made us safer, we'd be invincible now.

But demands for extreme safety and comfort — namely from a privileged minority living in wealthy suburbs as well as in cozy rural communities — tend to come at the expense of the majority and remain a luxury we can't afford.

This is not to say that crime isn't an issue. It is. It's just strange that the folks least likely to confront daily violent crime want more police and more jails and harsher penalties while people who live in dangerous communities consistently seek jobs and police accountability.

In Kansas, we have about 6,000 people in county jails, primarily because they don't have bail money.

When you don't have bail money — to get out of jail, hire a lawyer, and participate in your own defense — you tend to get convicted. Also here in Kansas, we have almost 10,000 people in prison.

But this old "fear of crime" song still manages to pack electoral dance floors when desperate politicians need to move a crowd.

Nixon pulled this album from its jacket and played it in 1968, promising safe but frightened Americans a return to traditional values and an end to what he called lawlessness following summers of racial unrest from Los Angeles to Detroit to Newark.

Former President Trump played a similar selection at his inauguration portraying the U.S. as crime-ridden, despite the fact that according to FactCheck.org, the nation's violent crime rate in 2015 was less than half of what it was at its 1991 peak.

Does crime happen? Of course.

But Americans worry disproportionately about crime, in part because news media on the left and the right have irresponsibly prioritized it. Forced to fill news pages, websites and airwaves, news organizations lean into crime coverage, creating a distorted reality for audiences.

The constant demand for absolute safety feels like people standing on the shore watching a boat capsize, demanding life preservers while people actually in the water drown.

Crime also has become a dog whistle for race, a reliable tool to nudge safe but frightened voters to the polls. The constant demand for absolute safety feels like people standing on the shore watching a boat capsize, demanding life preservers while people actually in the water drown.

This obsession with extreme safety and comfort has bled into other civic discussions.

We caught glimpses of this during the faux critical race theory debate. Fears from parents that their children might experience discomfort hearing what happened to Black people in this country actually swept some fearmongers into office.

Similar fears drive attempts at book banning.

The safest people seem preoccupied to the point of neurosis with safety and comfort. If locking people up made us safer, we'd be invincible.

We see it in the constant attacks on a tiny handful of transgender female athletes. We already have rules governing these aspects of competition.

We see it in voter suppression efforts, where a powerful minority essentially says that they want everything calibrated to their comfort and that just isn't possible if too many people are allowed to vote.

We see it in cancel culture, too: "You said something I disagree with, so you're banished."

Comfort and privilege breed this kind of entitlement. Like bad tippers, they demand lavish courtesies, but offer paltry appreciation if any.

Another perspective on privilege is inequality, and that's key here. Some people in our society have so much while others have so little. Our brand of cruel, guardrail-free, low-road capitalism creates and depends on such inequality.

One indication that you might have too much is the gnawing and constant sense that some imagined person or group plots to take it away from you.

Perhaps that's why so many Americans stockpile guns or move into enormous suburban homes behind gates and walls. They stack enormous wealth. They drive giant SUVs. They have so much that any movement toward equity feels like loss.

All this safety and comfort has made people soft. People have lost their sense of proportion. They've become what one pundit calls "emotional hemophiliacs."

All this fear has driven absolutely craven policies that continue to destroy lives, families and communities. Our society's only hope is to begin backing away from reflexive fear.

Three wise women have offered thoughts on a path forward.

Brene' Brown said, "you can choose courage, or you can choose comfort, but you cannot choose both."

Mary Tyler Moore said, "you can't be brave if you've only had wonderful things happen to you."

Maya Angelou perhaps said it best: "Without courage, we cannot practice any other virtue with consistency. We can't be kind, true, merciful, generous or honest."

So, fear not. It does more harm than good. Everything else we do is a choice.

34/ Isn't the world mean enough already?

June 24, 2025 published in *The Journal: A Civic Issues Magazine*

Many if not most Wichitans shuddered as news broke of the midair collision of American Airlines Flight 5342 with an Army Black Hawk helicopter on Jan. 29 – Kansas Day. More than likely in this place where six degrees of separation feel more like two degrees, we knew someone on that plane.

Reports hours later confirmed the worst. No survivors.

As shock morphed into grief, as search and rescue gave way to recovery, as fears turned to verification, suggestions that diversity programs had contributed to the disaster wafted from a White House news conference and from the state's junior senator.

Why, during such profound national grief, would anyone suggest such a thing?

The world is mean enough already. Why are so many hellbent on making it meaner?

That question is coming from someone who hates the standard kumbaya moments following most public tragedies and the loathsome we're-all-in-this-together platitudes that ignore obvious and intentional social stratifications.

But we now have beer-muscle influencers clamoring for get-tough measures while whining at the slightest inconveniences.

The socially permissive are enjoying the suffering of people believed to have voted for the candidate who'd hurt people, only to now find themselves hurting.

As satisfying as this may feel, they should choose to extend the empathy those folks were prepared to deny others.

The world is mean enough already.

Consider the changes wrought so far and the plight of the vulnerable: threats to Medicaid; food spoiling in ports while thousands starve; ending efforts to reunite children ripped away from undocumented parents.

It has felt like cruelty for cruelty's sake.

Those DEI comments felt particularly cruel because I knew the family of someone on that D.C.-bound plane, Kiah Duggins.

Kiah's father, Maurice, was my mother's doctor. Kiah's mom, Gwen, grew up in my childhood neighborhood, and her best friend was the older sister of my best friend. Realizing Kiah was on that plane felt so close and so personal.

They're the sort of people upon which strong communities are built. Kind, caring people who selflessly serve their community with no expectation of a spotlight. People the least deserving of having their loss politicized.

Weeks before, I'd asked Dr. Duggins to speak at a Black Legislative Day event featuring a proclamation from Gov. Laura Kelly and presentations from community advocates.

After learning that Kiah was on that plane, I can remember wishing it was not so and then looking at my bookshelf, and there among family photos, I saw a picture of Kiah.

It was on the cover of a hardback book of photos I'd published for Kansas African American Museum donors from our annual Tribute to Trailblazers gala. There she stood, smiling radiantly, a fist dug into her hip, and a vivid life of achievement ahead and behind her. I asked, Why must life be so cruel?

There's little we can do about tragic circumstances. Everything else we do is a choice.

35/ "Broad Sympathy for *Some*"

September 14, 2023

Possibly the best definition of modern racism came from journalist and author Ta-Nehisi Coates, who described it as "broad sympathy for some, broad skepticism of others."

This axiom came to mind recently during an email exchange with a private school administrator who seemed unbothered by secretly recorded comments his basketball coach, Mitch Fiegel, made about a biracial student athlete and his family. In the recording, coach said he wouldn't touch that "family with a 10-foot pole," and that he didn't "believe the student was a good person."

So, what's a dealbreaker? What goes too far? I considered the coach's behavior a dealbreaker. The school and the Kansas State High School Athletic Association did not. Wichita Collegiate officials and the state's high school athletics governing body have expressed "regret" for the championship coach's remarks, made while speaking to a caller claiming to work as a Georgetown University assistant coach.

Schools and KSHSAA hold players accountable, herding them in front of virtually all-white panels. But both entities seemed unwilling or uninterested in holding this coach accountable. Worse, they didn't inform the student or his parents.

This lack of accountability, transparency, and ethics indicates the need for vigorous reform, including greater diversity at KSHSAA, greater scrutiny of coaches, more transparency and more appellate options.

*Near the end
of the game,
he took a
victory bow
in front of
his old coach
and was
suspended
for the first
half of the
next game.*

I contacted the student's father, whom I know well. He declined to comment, citing legal advice. The father said neither Collegiate nor KSHSAA contacted him about the recording.

A few years ago, the student athlete played for Fiegel before transferring and later facing his old coach in a substate playoff game. The player carried his new team to a win. Near the end of the game, he took a victory bow in front of his old coach and was suspended for the first half of the next game.

Later, someone phoned Fiegel claiming to be a recruiter for Georgetown University and asked for an evaluation of the student athlete.

Fiegel said, "But deep down, do I believe he's a good kid from a good family? I wouldn't touch them with a 10-foot pole."

The caller later asked whether the student was a "good kid."

Said Fiegel: "Let me tell you what he did. … He came over in front of my bench and bowed. In front of me. And everybody saw it. I have never had anybody do anything like that in 35 years of coaching."

In another indication he knew he was harming the student, Fiegel said: "My name comes up in this, I'll be so pissed I can't see straight. I need to be done with this family, done with this kid."

He again targets the student.

"I wish I could tell you this kid was a great human being, but I don't believe that. I wish I did," Fiegel said on the recording.

Not the most vicious attack ever, but enough to do reputational damage. Today, this student is a college basketball player who mulled standout academic offers from Baylor, Oklahoma, Southern Methodist University, the University of Kansas, Kansas State University and Wichita State University.

I'm guessing they thought he was a good kid from a good family.

Still, the explanatory emailed comments from Collegiate and from the executive director of KSHSAA seemed more focused on the kid than on the coach.

For example, Collegiate's head of school Nathan Washer said the student "ran directly in front of our bench and our coach and taunted him in a manner that shocked all who witnessed it."

Actually, video doesn't show the student running to the bench. The player had just been standing there.

A bow seems benign, compared to that description that seemed designed to make the coach's comments more palatable. In a sports culture that has moved from "It's not whether you win or lose it's how you play the game," to, "in your face!" a bow isn't shocking.

Washer said: "It is clear … that this call was set up by someone to try and lead coach Fiegel into saying something negative about the student in question. This is a case of a coach referring to the behavior of this particular student and is not a pattern of behavior as your earlier questions suggest."

Washer didn't mention that Fiegel barely survived an ouster campaign in recent years.

KSHSAA executive director Bill Faflick said his office "has had nothing recent relative to coach Fiegel or Wichita Collegiate School. Several years ago, we did get an anonymous communication (mailing with voice memo, no return address or name attached)."

Faflick said: "Consistent with our anonymous communication protocol, the information was sent to the school for review. ... The concern had nothing to do with KSHSAA rules, nor was a safety risk referenced or inferred. I do not believe an athlete's name was included in the voice memo (the last name was used). It was an issue that would fall under local school purview."

So, neither entity considered Fiegel's words a dealbreaker.

This essentially proves my point that both entities need more diverse voices. Fiegel still works for Collegiate. This feels like a coverup. What we allow, it seems, we endorse.

Fiegel received broad sympathy. The student, broad skepticism. Typically, the Black child endured harsher punishment. He deserved at worst a technical for the bow, but a conversation on the bench could have sufficed. The half-game suspension reflected Fiegel's caste status, not the bow.

Greater diversity in the system creates more people who would understand and sympathize with the travails of Black athletes.

We (myself and my editors) have decided not to identify the student nor embed audio from the call. We did this to protect the student.

I only wish these institutions had sympathized more with the student, rather than circling the wagons around a thin-skinned coach.

[Historical note: Star Black athletes Eddie Thomas and Oscar Jones, who would graduate from Wichita high schools in the late 1960s, recall being prevented from playing their senior year because coaches claimed they could not play so many Black players.]

36/ Let's Redefine Freedom as Parity

June 19, 2022 published in *Community Voices*

As we approach our second Juneteenth national holiday, the nation should ponder its definition of freedom. The holiday marks the moment in time when enslaved people in Texas learned they'd been freed from one type of bondage.

But by virtually every social and economic measurement, African Americans have in succession traded one form of bondage for another, from chattel slavery to convict leasing, to sharecropping, to Jim Crow, to today's mass incarceration.

This Juneteenth, African Americans should consider a new standard for freedom — economic parity. A dear friend, Dr. Pamela Jolly, the CEO of Torch Enterprises, has supported this kind of metric for years. Real parity, she said, begins with understanding our individual and collective contributions to building economic power.

Juneteenth marks the end of American chattel slavery. The name originates from June 19, 1865, when Maj. Gen. Gordon Granger in Texas announced that "all slaves are free." Months later, the 13th Amendment abolished bondage slavery, though slavery for the incarcerated continues today.

But releasing people from bondage and later declaring an end to government-sanctioned discrimination did not address the 12 generations of legal and social constructs that destroyed most existing or fledgling African American wealth.

Wealth building in the Black community is Jolly's expertise and the subject of her dissertation. Leveraging her findings, she created the Narrow Road, and has written five books on the subject.

Jolly, a graduate of the Wharton School of Business and Boston University's School of Theology, has worked as a credit analyst, a vice president of treasury management, and helped launch financial initiatives designed to educate and inform about the critical role of legacy wealth in the Black community and ways to pursue it. She has hosted legacy wealth cohorts in cities nationwide. She has lectured in Korea, Egypt, Nigeria, Jamaica, China and England.

Her firm's name, Torch Enterprises, references passing the torch of wealth from one generation to another. Since emancipation, the African American journey toward cross-generational wealth has met with systemic roadblocks. Gaps formed and grew, and not just financial ones.

If Black voters and white voters don't have comparable wait times at the polls on Election Day, that's not parity. If the groups aren't harassed, and jailed at comparable rates, that's not parity. If our schools don't produce comparable outcomes, that's not parity.

The financial parity challenge involves advancing strategies that narrow the racial wealth gap and measure our progress. According to the Brookings Institution, the typical white family had nearly 10 times the wealth of a Black family in 2016.

Thomas Shapiro and others have identified specific actions to accelerate the narrowing of the gap, opening the doors of opportunity for individual wealth journeys.

If Black voters and white voters don't have comparable wait times at the polls on Election Day, that's not parity.

Parity offers a path forward because racial wealth inequality is 90% structural, Jolly said.

"I really want us to recognize that we have inherited this unique time in history to work on our individual and collective progress to make this happen," she said. "Every fourth generation repeats itself. We have inherited the spirit and intention of the generations who rebuilt Tulsa and other cities across this country. This is our time."

After concerted generational efforts, in the late 1980s, Asian Americans, Jolly said, reached entrepreneurial parity with white Americans. Their median income and net worth surpassed that of white Americans.

"Parity enables us to set a definitive marker," she said. "Then, we can turn that definitive marker into a series of cross-generational steps to get further down the road to wealth."

Individual economic parity yields sustainable community outcomes. But this requires us to increase our awareness of where we are on the road to generational wealth.

"Wealth is a group process," Jolly said. "Working together toward wealth outcomes you believe you can have a bloc, a tax base, contributing to the broader society while it is also building wealth for you. I call that a win-win."

She has found that it takes three generations to build legacy wealth. When four generations stay financially connected, the wealth wheel begins to turn, setting a standard for future generations. Unifying behind an inclusive plan is how we can remember Juneteenth as a time in our shared history when the delayed notice of freedom had to end.

"It just takes one generation going it alone to lose the opportunity to build legacy wealth," she warned.

Jolly ultimately hopes to establish 40 "Torch" cities nationally.

She wrote her doctoral dissertation on the Biblical exodus from the financial wilderness to the inherited Promised Land. It noted how the Levites were the only tribe to not receive a Promised Land inheritance. The Levites did, however, receive 10% from each tribe they used to create cities of refuge.

"I desire to create 40 cities of financial refuge," she said. "Centered in Black communities. I want to co-create closed-loop economic circles whose pursuit of parity builds infrastructure that is culturally relevant to the residents living there. Where, if you can't navigate your way to wealth in the financial wilderness by yourself, you could find your way to one of these places and find your promise and build wealth your way."

In an era where debt is a new form of slavery, Jolly seems to have the key to our shackles. Our racial wealth gap threatens our democracy, just as general inequality threatens democracy. Individuals can't compete with wealthy people colluding with politicians.

Parity offers the truer path to freedom for African Americans and to a healthier democracy.

Juneteenth's emancipation remembrance merely marks the first step.

Months later, the 13th Amendment abolished bondage slavery, though slavery for the incarcerated continues today.

37/ No One Should Settle for "a piece of freedom"

January 15, 2023

Some historians mark the Rev. Martin Luther King Jr.'s murder as the end of the civil rights movement. Over an arc of 14 years — from the 1954 *Brown* Decision to King's death in 1968 — the nation attempted to address its racial caste system.

The same nation that launched a war on hunger and a war on poverty and pursued a Great Society, however, elected Ronald Reagan president just 12 years after King's death and ushered in a new era of conservatism, bent on rolling back racial advancements and dismantling Great Society efforts.

This push and pull have resulted in the kind of gradualism and tokenism King warned about, especially the pantomime that passes for civil rights advancement efforts today. Until we do away with tokenism, the structures of privilege reflexively protecting status quo inequality will persist.

King tackled this issue in a 1962 speech, equating tokenism to stall tactics.

"A new and hastily constructed roadblock has appeared in the form of planned and institutionalized tokenism," King said. "We have advanced in some places from all-out, unrestrained resistance to a sophisticated form of delaying tactics, embodied in tokenism."

This stood as "one of the most difficult problems that the integration movement confronts," he said.

"A piece of freedom," King continued, "is no longer enough for human beings nor for the nation of which Negroes are part. They have been given pieces — but unlike bread, a slice of liberty does not finish hunger. Freedom is like life. It cannot be had in installments. Freedom is indivisible — we have it all or we are not free."

Consider how the fight for equality has progressed in the past 60 years. Moving goal posts. Changing rules. Willful ignorance.

Incrementalism is resistance.

Integrate public pools, and then watch people fill them with cement and open private pools behind gates or walls in exclusive communities.

Integrate public schools or a neighborhood, and watch people flee to suburbs and open private schools. Today, many legislatures continue to try funneling public money into those private schools.

Gain the right to vote, then watch politicians alter voting districts, demand birth certificates and rip out drop boxes.

Also a part of today's tokenism? Breathlessly describing any education about the integration of pools or schools or neighborhoods or any classroom discussion about the denial of voting rights as Critical Race Theory or wokeism.

On these issues, King reigns as a man who saw tomorrow. What's terrifying is how relentless this tokenism remains.

Herschel Walker's Senate campaign comes to mind. Black conservatives often get trotted out to weigh in on racial issues that affect wide swaths of the Black citizenry, but those appointed spokespeople represent maybe 10 to 15 percent of that bloc.

That doesn't make them illegitimate. They just aren't at all representative of a preponderance of Black thought. Representative samples remain the norm, except here.

Such gradualism may prove dangerous. King warned of that in a separate speech, saying "this is no time to engage in the luxury of cooling off or to take the tranquilizing drug of gradualism."

We must call gradualism what it is: A struggle to maintain the right to deny people rights you enjoy. Gradualism means that you'll get what I think you deserve when I'm comfortable.

King says as much in his book, *Where Do We Go from Here: Chaos or Community?*

"Negroes have proceeded from the premise that equality means what it says, and they have taken white Americans at their word when they talk of it as an objective. But most whites in America … proceed from a premise that equality is a loose expression for improvement. White America is not even psychologically organized to close the gap — essentially, it seeks only to make it less painful, less obvious but in most respects, to retain it."

It should startle us that someone with his capacity for patience and love arrived at this determination.

But considering the January 6, 2021, insurrection, the wealth and opportunity hoarding, the cries of "I want my country back!" or "Make America great again" (as the Ku Klux Klan once declared), the continued whitewashing of history, the increasing abandonment of democratic norms — was King wrong?

King was tired of tokenism more than 50 years ago. Shouldn't we dispense with token efforts at achieving equality?

We must call gradualism what it is: A struggle to maintain the right to deny people rights you enjoy. Gradualism means that you'll get what I think you deserve when I'm comfortable.

Justice delayed is justice denied.

Let's not overthink this. King has done the heavy lifting and thinking here: If you don't want liberty for absolutely everyone, you don't love liberty. You love your privilege.

38/ "Thing-Oriented" Versus Human Needs

October 13, 2023

It takes concentration not to see certain realities — the mother holding the handwritten sign at the traffic light; the man sleeping under a bridge; the tent cities on public right of ways.

But we make the effort.

In downtown Kansas City, developers plan an entertainment district with a Ferris wheel centerpiece. There's also talk of a new baseball stadium downtown. A $160 million park built on top of Interstate-670 downtown waits on the horizon.

We routinely look past the obvious suffering of neighbors to find millions for selfish wants that will do nothing to address any kind of suffering. This happens in most communities. The desire for amusements has supplanted any desire to meet actual human needs.

Given our inability to curb such spending, we should demand dollar-for-dollar spending on social uplift for every dollar spent on Ferris wheels, dog parks or sports venues. Otherwise, the extravagances will continue unabated, and the needy will continue to disappear from our priority lists.

In the 1990s, as spasms of gang violence terrorized Little Rock, Arkansas, that city passed a one-cent sales tax and vowed to spend a dollar on prevention for every dollar spent on suppression. Every new prosecutor or patrolman hire meant more money for needs as well as for wants.

Other cities should try this, even if it begins with a moratorium on popular public amenity projects unless and until there's sufficient money to address needs such as public violence or homelessness. Maybe we could leech some of the guilt from these guilty pleasure projects.

Maybe this idea persuades cities to stop chasing the pipe dream that somehow American tourists will stop caring about beaches and mountains and start choosing Kansas or Missouri as prime vacation spots.

Maybe those enrichment packages get smaller, saving taxpayers money.

Maybe we claw back some ground we've ceded to the developers who always seem to be in line for a public money handout.

The Rev. Martin Luther King Jr. once argued that global warfare spending stymied "programs of social uplift." We needed to shift from a "thing-oriented" society to a person-oriented society, King said.

"When machines and computers, profit motives and property rights are considered more important than people, the giant triplets of racism, materialism and militarism are incapable of being conquered," he said.

We're still choosing "things" over people.

Chase Billingham, an associate professor of sociology, studies this phenomenon. Billingham said cities enter negotiations with developers at a decided disadvantage. Multiple cities compete against each other for projects. Ultimately, the cities give away the store to secure deals, he said.

When machines and computers, profit motives and property rights are considered more important than people, the giant triplets of racism, materialism and militarism are incapable of being conquered

– The Rev. Martin Luther King Jr.

It's complicated, Billingham said.

City officials could argue that some citizens do want these vanity projects and that the city needs them to generate funds necessary to fight social problems.

"A lot of people like going to sporting events," Billingham said. "They like going to the farmers market. They like going to the park, and they like having new and shiny things in their city. And especially young people — people we might call gentrifiers — asking for that new kind of development.

"So, there's political pressure on city council members and mayors and city managers to produce those new kinds of consumer amenities that are oriented toward the consumption tastes of the middle and upper class. And those people are more likely to vote."

Also, Billingham said, there's money in development and no money in addressing homelessness.

By now, we ought to understand that the violence, the homelessness and the inequality in our communities have deeper origins than poor choices. Systems and processes help maintain violence, widespread homelessness and uneven opportunity.

Community leaders tend to mention poverty only during election years or when questioned why they're funding new hotels and stadiums instead of pocked roads, crumbling schools and tent cities.

We haven't fully funded schools. We support juvenile courts on the backs of kids and poor families. We don't have parity in spending between district attorneys and public defenders. Foster kids still need more.

Why are we building professional ball stadiums? Why do we make sure the wealthy have more than they need while insisting that the poor get less than

Why do we make sure the wealthy have more than they need while insisting that the poor get less than they need?

they need? We make this calculation each time we choose the frivolous over the substantive.

Blissful unawareness remains our societal default.

If author James Baldwin is to be believed, it's a conscious choice masquerading as a subconscious one. To maintain this level of comfort, we can't afford to pay attention.

"For a very long time, America prospered," Baldwin said. "This prosperity cost millions of people their lives. Now, not even the people who are the most spectacular recipients of the benefits of this prosperity, are able to endure these benefits. They can neither understand them nor do without them … they cannot imagine the price paid by their victims or subjects for this way of life, and so they cannot afford to know why the victims are revolting.

"This is a formula for nation or kingdom decline."

Yes, we have an answer to the question: "What to get the neighbor who has nothing?"

Apparently, *more* public amenities.

39/ Critical Race Theory's Only Error: Its Name

June 8, 2021 published in *Community Voices*

The late historian John Henrik Clarke explained the dominant subculture's preoccupation with manipulating history.

Europeans "began manipulating history in the 15th century to justify the slave trade," said Clarke, a pioneer in Pan-African studies, during an interview with Tony Brown on Brown's eponymous show in the 1970s.

Modern racism incubated during this period, Clarke said.

Detractors of critical race theory — a catch-all for the study of American history and institutions as extensions of racial injustice that influence law, the economy and culture — embody Clarke's explanation. Kansas Attorney General Derek Schmidt among them.

What needed hiding, essentially from our founding to today? Much of what critical race theory opponents still want hidden. It's gruesome, but it's our history.

Most of us learned, for example, about slave traders and slave owners, but never about slave breakers, who employed ghastly means to break the spirits of enslaved Africans.

Slave breakers tortured husbands to death in front of pregnant wives, hoping to not only break the spirit of the woman but intending to funnel fear into the unborn child. Slave breakers also sliced the unborn from their mother's wombs and killed them in front of their fathers.

"You cannot enslave a man and say he is a human being," Clarke said.

The American Slave Trade by John R. Spears, *From Slavery to Freedom* by John Hope Franklin, *The Negro Family in the United States* by E. Franklin Frazier, *Antislavery* by Dwight Lowell Dumond, and *Malcolm X on Afro-American History* all reference this process.

Could a society justifying *this* actually grant Black people equal rights?

It hasn't, and attacking critical race theory offers ways to justify racial wealth and health gaps and other forms of socially engineered inequality.

Slavery begat sharecropping and convict leasing, during which people who'd been systematically denied jobs were arrested for vagrancy, imprisoned, and then worked to death.

African Americans endured segregation and a period of lynching that extended deep into the 20th century. Throngs attended lynchings. Some collected the victims' skin and teeth as souvenirs. Others made postcards of the spectacle.

The Tulsa race massacre of 1921 wasn't an outlier. Similar incidents happened in places like Wilmington, North Carolina, and Springfield, Missouri.

That period gave way to housing discrimination.

Our government offered loans to white families moving from urban housing projects to new homes in publicly funded suburbs. Black families were explicitly denied such loans and couldn't escape to better schools or build wealth through home ownership as the emerging white middle class did.

Richard Rothstein's *The Color of Law* expertly detailed these practices, explaining that current housing patterns aren't an accident but the result of explicit government policy.

The bipartisan *Kerner Commission Report* in 1968 addressed these housing patterns.

Race remains an organizing principle in America. Any racial reckoning requires an understanding of this fundamental fact.

"What white Americans have never fully understood — but what the Negro can never forget — is that white society is deeply implicated in the ghetto," the report read. "White institutions created it, white institutions maintain it, and white society condones it."

Those housing patterns still frustrate efforts at school integration and educational equality.

Many Americans are rightfully ashamed of this history. Others who don't know — or who don't care to know — are the people angered by Colin Kaepernick and others pursuing critical race theory-driven discussions.

But attempts by Schmidt and others to hide this history are misguided.

How do you evade prosecution for a crime?

Silence the witnesses.

Critical race theory's only error is its name. It isn't a theory at all. It represents the lived Black experience. And I haven't mentioned red-lining, environmental racism (Flint, Michigan), police terror, mass incarceration or how the government typically rammed interstate highways through Black communities.

Race remains an organizing principle in America. Any racial reckoning requires an understanding of this fundamental fact. From the Three-fifths Compromise, to the U.S. Supreme Court's Dred Scott ruling that enslaved people had "no rights the white man was bound to respect," to today.

Yes, we've revised the Constitution and no, Scott is no longer precedent. But there's much more to do and critical race theory is a part of that healing process.

We don't arrive at truth until suffering speaks.

Critical race theory opponents — some of whom also are whitewashing the Jan. 6 insurrection — want to keep their knees on truth's neck, hoping to silence the horrors and suffering of the past.

The maintenance of our current status quo depends on it.

40/ Does Calvinism Explain America's White Evangelical Movement?

December 2, 2025

Kansas Interfaith Action members participate in a demonstration on May 20, 2025, outside the federal courthouse in Topeka, where they protested Core Civic and the for-profit detention of immigrants. (Sherman Smith/ Kansas Reflector)

As of late last year, more than 1,300 children torn from their parents' arms at the U.S.–Mexico border from 2017 to 2021 had not been reunited with their parents. This figure represents nearly a third of the 4,600 children forcibly separated from their families.

Human rights organizations described this as potentially a form of torture, due to the intentional infliction of suffering and the systemic nature of the separations as an immigration deterrent.

Such measures enjoyed support and even celebration from the American Christian right, leaving many to wonder: What kind of religion endorses such cruelty, the withholding of health care, winking at racism and embracing xenophobia?

There's little Christian about this, it seems, unless viewed through a theologically Calvinist lens.

The Rev. Robert Johnson, who leads Church of the Resurrection's new Lee's Summit location, said the seeming detachment from suffering, tolerance of destructive ideas like "Manifest Destiny" and more likely have Calvinist roots.

"In their minds, God has already chosen," said Johnson, who earlier led a United Methodist Church in Wichita. "Social justice is viewed as impudence to God's executed will, and it's also anti-empathy. In fact, empathy is meaningless."

In August, PBS News published a story headlined, "Is Empathy A Sin? Some Conservative Christians Argue It Can Be."

Reverend Robert Johnson
(Submitted photo)

"For them, empathy is a cudgel for the left," the article explained. "It can manipulate caring people into accepting all manner of sins according to a conservative Christian perspective, including abortion access, LGBTQ+ rights, illegal immigration and certain views on social and racial justice."

Allie Beth Stuckey, author of *Toxic Empathy: How Progressives Exploit Christian Compassion*, was quoted as saying: "Empathy becomes toxic when it encourages you to affirm sin, validates lies or supports destructive policies."

Christian right beliefs have buttressed political conservatism for decades, from the Confederacy's "Lost Cause," to Jerry Falwell's "Moral Majority," to today's MAGA movement. Falwell's Liberty University didn't originally admit Black students. To be fair, not all evangelicals hold such beliefs, but we should try to understand where the beliefs of so many might come from.

A review of Anthea Butler's *White Evangelical Racism: The Politics of Morality in America*, by Bianca Mabute-Louie, identifies evangelicalism as a nationalist political movement to support white, Christian hegemony. Racism is a feature, not a bug, of the movement.

Butler, according to Mabute-Louie, said, "interpretation of Scriptures, theology, and belief informed evangelicals' social and political actions, and justified the oppression of African Americans during and post-enslavement."

Many Americans have been puzzled by evangelicals' devotion to President Donald Trump despite his lurid personal peccadillos, his seeming lack of religiosity and the cruelty of his recent attempt to deny millions, including children, of food benefits.

Christians and non-Christians alike have asked earnestly how any believer — left, right or otherwise — could support such policies and such a person.

Johnson suggested these beliefs reach deep into 1500-era teachings of John Calvin and "predestination."

Most students learned about Calvinism from a historical, not religious, perspective. The Pilgrims, for example, were Calvinists. That's also where the "Protestant work ethic" originated, as well as interpretations of the Bible as "without error."

Calvin believed that "even before creation," God had chosen some people for salvation, a belief associated with predestination. Calvin fumed at how Catholicism reduced religion to "salvation by works."

His refrain? People shouldn't try to manipulate God nor place Him in their debt. Saved people are saved only by Him, not by good works.

To be fair, not all evangelicals hold such beliefs.

"This is the perfect theology for what we see in the evangelical movement," Johnson said. "This is why they may not consider themselves bigoted or racist. They have found a denominational justification for our racial caste system. It's why they don't like social activism. To them, there is no social Gospel, only individual salvation."

Johnson pointed to the acronym TULIP for understanding.

TULIP stands for total depravity (there's no good in us), unconditional election (God has already chosen those who prosper), limited atonement (Jesus died specifically for the elect), and perseverance of the saints (the elect will be saved).

John Wesley, a founder of modern Methodism, provided an alternative to this theology for many, including for Johnson.

Wesley, Johnson said, looked at slavery and like Calvin, saw total depravity. But Wesley also saw God in the tortured enslaved people and heard an ecclesiastical call to rescue them.

"From his deathbed, John Wesley pleaded with people gathered around him to promise to end the scourge of slavery," Johnson said. "I follow United Methodism in that spirit."

A photo of a crying toddler caught up in a nighttime border raid remains an enduring image from the first Trump administration's "zero tolerance" immigration policy.

The prolonged family separation stemmed from the federal government's failure to maintain a central database. A 2018 court order halted the practice, and a 2023 settlement requires continued reunification efforts and support through 2031.

But a lifetime of damage already has been done, especially to the children. Pope Leo has called out the "extremely disrespectful" treatment of migrants in the U.S., according to an NPR report.

The question then becomes not if God exists in the crying toddler or her parents, but where is God in a faith tradition that embraces such wanton and intentional cruelty?

41/ Gossip Haunted Kansas Man after Missouri Officials' False Claims

October 15, 2025

There is a scene in the 2008 film *Doubt*, set in a 1964 Catholic grade school, where the priest told a story about a woman gossiping about a man she hardly knew — a situation Denton Loudermill Jr. understood when he was falsely accused in the 2024 shooting at the Kansas City Chiefs celebratory parade.

Missouri officials falsely accused Denton Loudermill Jr. in a fatal 2024 shooting at the Kansas City Chiefs Super Bowl parade. Gossip haunted his last days. (Submitted)

In the movie, the woman dreamed that night of a great hand appearing that pointed down at her. Seized with an overwhelming sense of guilt, she went to confession the next day with the parish priest, Father O'Rourke.

"Is gossiping a sin?" she asked. "Was that the hand of God almighty pointing a finger at me? Should I be asking your absolution, Father? Tell me, have I done something wrong?"

"Yes," the priest said. "You've borne false witness against your neighbor. You played fast and loose with his reputation, and you should be heartily ashamed."

Gossip haunted Loudermill in his last days with technologically supercharged rumor traveling at light speed, leading to death threats and slander from which he, and his family, could not escape.

People may not remember his name, but his family will never forget how people falsely accused him in a shooting that claimed one life and injured 22, including children.

He'd stood dazed in the chaos.

People screamed. Fight or flight hormones activated. Panicked parents scooped up little ones as best they could and sought safety, not knowing if they were running at or away from danger.

Unlike those who ran, Loudermill froze, said LaRonna Lassiter Saunders, part of the legal team representing Loudermill's family.

"He saw a woman shot and bleeding out," she said. "The shooting began near him. He was in shock. Everyone started running, but he asked himself, 'Where should I run?' He was waiting for his ride to pick him up."

Public torment for this intensely private man began here.

Police cuffed him and sat him on a curb where people began photographing him, perhaps assuming police had collared one of the shooters. Police stopped Loudermill, Lassiter Saunders said, because he moved slowly.

Hard to blame the police in this context. This doesn't seem malicious. Still, Loudermill sat helpless as photos of him traversed the internet like a lit fuse about to detonate and destroy his carefully guarded world. It did.

Someone at an undisclosed website posted the picture and labeled him a "terrorist," and an illegal immigrant. Those images and that narrative spread like a virus. Two Missouri officials used the photo in posts urging the president to "close the border."

U.S. Chief Magistrate Judge Willie J. Epps Jr. on October 7 allowed Loudermill's defamation case against Missouri Secretary of State Denny Hoskins and state Sen. Rick Brattin to proceed.

Emails sent to the offices of Hoskins and Brattin were not answered.

Given the appetite in wide swaths of society to allow masked law enforcement to tackle and shackle foreign-looking people, imagine the impact on Loudermill and his family.

Death threats rose like a flood.

"I'm just a light-skinned Black dude," Lassiter Saunders recalled Loudermill saying. "Why are they lying on me? I was born and raised in Olathe. I've been here all my life."

This digital mob predictably but painfully took its toll.

His counselor diagnosed him with post-traumatic stress disorder. In conversations with Lassiter Saunders, he wondered if he'd survive. His weight crashed, leaving him unrecognizable.

"This happened often, usually at the beginning of our conversations," she said. "The first part of my representation, I was like a counselor."

Loudermill, she said, would see references to the parade shooting on television. He rarely ventured into social media, but his children would see threats and accusations about him.

Once, at work, he told her he saw someone staring at him. He said they punched keys on their phone. It seemed as though they were pulling up his photo and when it appeared, it registered on their faces.

Once the digital mob poured the illegal alien and terrorist narrative into a mold, it quickly hardened into a truth-resistant bulwark of gossip and stupidity.

"This cost him his life," Lassiter Saunders said. "The process has outlived him."

His family found him dead on April 11.

There seems no remedy sufficient for what happened to him. To date, she said, the officials who wrongfully posted his photo have not apologized.

In *Doubt*, the gossiping woman did say she was sorry and asked for forgiveness.

"Not so fast," Father O'Rourke said.

He ordered her to go home, take a pillow from her bed, climb to her roof, and cut it open.

The woman did as the priest asked and returned.

"What was the result?" he asked.

"Feathers," she said. "Feathers everywhere, father."

"Now, I want you to go back and gather up every last feather that flew out on the wind," he said.

"It can't be done," she said. "I don't know where they went. The wind took them all over."

"And that," O'Rourke said sharply, "is gossip."

And for many, the image of this innocent man as some immigrant terrorist still floats on the digital four winds, impervious to truth.

42/ Grief and Uncertainty Can Be a Bond

September 24, 2025 published in *The Journal: A Civics Issues Magazine.*

John Patrick Shanley opened a dialogue in his acclaimed Catholic school movie drama *Doubt*, set in 1964, with a homily juxtaposing public grief and private pain. Philip Seymour Hoffman, portraying Father Brendan Flynn asks his flock, "What do you do when you're not sure?"

The marquee of Barleycorn's club in Wichita conveys the grief of a community mourning the Kansans and other passengers and crew killed in a Washington D.C. plane and helicopter crash last week. (Hugo Phan/KMUW)

"Last year when President Kennedy was assassinated, who among us did not experience the most profound disorientation." Hoffman's character asked. "Despair. Which way? What now? What do I say to my kids? What do I tell myself?"

It poses grief's suffocating question: Is this more than I can bear? This remains a question many in Wichita now face through three seasons of grievous loss.

As winter laid down across a cold, January night, a Wichita-to-Washington, D.C., flight collided in midair with an Army Blackhawk helicopter and plunged into the freezing Potomac River. The icy morning sun bore the worst possible news for many Wichitans: the loss of Kiah Duggins, a young Harvard University law school graduate and daughter to two community pillars.

In August as summer's scorching began to fade, a dual tragedy. An 80-year-old woman accused of speeding, alcohol impairment and running a red light T-boned a car carrying LaShea Capri Bell and her daughter, A'Niah. The mother and daughter died at the scene. A'Niah planned to apply to medical school.

LaShea Capri Bell and her daughter, A'Niah. (Courtesy)

Wedged between these tragedies in May's spring flowering, the community lost William "Buggs" Polite, a gifted Morehouse College graduate, an education advocate, a friend to all and masterful math tutor who, in what spare time he had, also visited and counseled incarcerated youths.

The loss of any one of the four contained ample grief for an entire year, but two-thirds of the way through 2025, anxiety haunts family and friends who question the fates, hold their breath and wonder how much more can they take.

Kiah would have turned 31 in September. A'Niah died at 25. Both now rest haloed by all their shining potential, by what they'd never become. LaShea, 41, and Buggs, 58, served the community in many ways but won't finish their most important work.

All served Wichita. LaShea served as a volunteer, Buggs as a stalwart in public education, and Kiah and A'Niah as striking examples of the supernova talent the city can produce.

But consider these losses in a more concentrated way for the small African American community from whence they emerged, and the hurt defies boundaries. These lives bordered so many others that whether you knew them or not, you still felt the shock waves.

"It's overwhelming on so many levels," said Marquetta Atkins-Woods, an executive of the nonprofit Destination Innovation, a youth empowerment organization. "Why is God selecting some of His best for these departures?"

Atkins Woods knew Kiah, whom she described as an "unafraid ball of fire," but was closer to Kiah's mom, Gwen. Atkins-Woods said her daughter idolized Kiah and used her success as a kind of scholastic and professional compass.

"The world is so loud now, and losing your baby has to be deafening," Atkins-Woods said. "One of the things you have to do is hold onto your light. Kiah was an embodiment of that."

She acknowledged the wounded community might not be at full capacity for that, however.

"I think about Dr. Polite, LaShea, Lynn Gilkey (a nonprofit executive who lost her son a few years ago), people who have dedicated their lives … to youth and young people and the fact that you gave your life to being a mentor. There's a lot of sacrifice in that work. Their rosters are filled with different young people whose lives they've touched.

"Then to lose your life or your own child. That part is heaviest on my mind."

Father Flynn compared that sort of individual grief to the collective.

"It was a time of people sitting together, bound together, by a common feeling of hopelessness," Father Flynn said of the Kennedy assassination. "But think of that. Your bond with your fellow being was your despair. It was a public experience. It was awful. But we were in it together."

Pivoting, he said, "How much worse is it then for the lone man, the lone woman, stricken by a private calamity? 'No one knows I'm sick.' 'No one knows I've lost my last real friend.' 'No one knows I've done something wrong.' Imagine the isolation.

"Now you see the world as through a window. On one side of the glass, happy, untroubled people, and on the other side, you."

In a 2017 magazine interview, Houston-based grief counselor Asma Rehman described the wrenching merger of collective grief along with "anticipatory grief" as not only acknowledgment of the moment, but also the marsh of unresolved grief unfolding ahead.

"When whole communities start to experience collective and anticipatory grief, that feeling of being out of control can become stronger than ever," Rehman said. "When usually, we are only in tune with our own grieving and mourning processes, we're now linked and connected and in tune with the grief and mourning processes of others."

Assembling to mourn and grieve publicly, Rehman said, could affirm crucial communal ties.

Atkins Woods has seen efforts to emotionally manage these community losses. Gwen, for example, is carrying on Kiah's Princess Project and along with others, allowing Kiah's beacon to continue sweeping the sky, and hopefully, easing any doubts.

"We're talking about it," she said. "The conversations are being had on social (media), but we're having them. People are talking about building and rebuilding. Taking on that space (the work left behind). Just working together to keep that legacy alive and to thrive. It's different things for different people, but we are really working on processing it."

Atkins Woods is describing Ubuntu philosophy, essentially, "I am, because we are, and we are, because I am." Communities shape individuals, and individuals shape communities. These interactions offer an expression of a common good.

This kind of effort in working through uncertainty can lead to that unremitting question about the future, actually finding the means to answer itself.

It's not easy, though.

In his book *Between the World and Me*, Ta-Nehisi Coates offered a lengthy list of time, commitments, hopes and dreams people pour into loved ones and the reverberations when all those efforts get spilled.

"Think of all the love poured into him. Think of the tuitions for Montessori and music lessons. Think of the gasoline expended, the treads worn carting him to football games, basketball tournaments, and Little League. Think of the time spent regulating sleepovers. Think of the surprise birthday parties, the day care, and the reference checks on babysitters. Think of World Book and Childcraft. Think of checks written for family photos. Think of credit cards charged for vacations. Think of soccer balls, science kits, chemistry sets, racetracks, and the model trains. Think of all the embraces, all the private jokes, customs, greetings, names, dreams. All the shared knowledge and capacity of a Black family injected into that vessel of flesh and bone. And think of how that vessel was taken, shattered on the concrete, and all its holy contents, all that had gone into him, sent flowing back to earth."

The contents, though, can flow back to the community at first in grief, but also into the kind of hope and generosity that can be poured into the next Kiah, the next LaShea, the next A'Niah, the next Buggs.

Everyone knows how doubt feels, Father Flynn said, and that's the crucial connection.

"Doubt can be a bond as powerful and sustaining as certainty. When you are lost, you are not alone."

43/ Partisan Attacks on the Common Good

July 23, 2025

The U.S. Supreme Court last week ruled the Trump administration could continue dismantling the Department of Education. Waves of firings halted by a lower court could now resume, it seems, until all 1,400 employees are gone.

The department oversees billions for schools, for civil rights actions, for a federal student loan program, for education access. In other words, the common good.

It's the latest public institution under assault by people obsessed with destroying any semblance of a common good. This tension between America's soaring ideals and its cruel realities has existed as long as the country has.

Congress established the department back in 1979. Closing it not only would require an act of Congress, but likely supermajority votes. If this fight sounds familiar, it's because it has historical roots.

A June NPR podcast, "The First Department of Education," whisked listeners to the 1830s as a "common school movement" developed in the Northeast. Nativist fears about Irish Catholic immigrants propelled the effort.

Proponents believed education could reverse increasing societal fragmentation. This might help unify the country under a common system — free public school in every state — not just for education, but also for citizenship.

Future President James Garfield in 1866 called education one of government's most economical expenditures.

"A tenth of our national debt expended in public education 50 years ago would have saved us the blood and treasure of the late war," Garfield said, according to the podcast. "A far less sum may save our children from still greater calamity."

Congress created the department, but it lasted only about a year, dragged down by claims education represented a waste of money, that it undermined local control and that the word "education" didn't appear in the Constitution.

The South, according to the podcast, considered education dangerous. The Black population represented a majority or near majority in a handful of Southern states, and withholding education offered an effective means of social control.

The podcast also pointed out that Southerners seemed more vulnerable to demagoguery because of a lack of education.

Withholding education as social control fits a historical pattern. Any common good seemingly must weather accusations of wastefulness. This push for individualism benefits the wealthy minority at the expense of a hardscrabble majority.

The strategy crystallizes though today's performative cruelty. Crushing empathy is necessary to stamping out a sense of common good, whether education, voting rights, or universal health care (opposed by rich politicians on public health care).

Increasing waves of politicians exalt qualities that should disqualify them as public officials: a mistrust of government, demonizing opponents, and supporting private schools with public money. These qualities should stand as barriers to candidacy, not bona fides.

Countless candidates promote themselves as "CEOs," but governments aren't corporations. Governments exist for the common good.

Wichita State University associate professor of sociology Chase Billingham said this rugged individualism, marked by minimal social obligations, remains a bedrock principle for those leaning right.

He said the late British Prime Minister Margaret Thatcher once argued there was "no such thing as a society."

"Our government, our social safety net and some of our most treasured institutions, like public libraries, public schools and public media ... are all antithetical to that radical individualism," he said.

Such institutions represent a kind society, but they face extinction or significant weakening, he said. The result will be a society characterized by self-interest and self-centeredness — a mean society.

"Increasingly, treasured resources will be available exclusively to those who can pay for them," he said. And as we lurch toward Thatcher's ideal, "even the most ardent conservatives will find that they don't enjoy the actual experience of living in that world."

Until Gov. Laura Kelly ascended to Cedar Crest, Kansas routinely underfunded public education, and right now, extremists in the Legislature want to send public money into private schools via school vouchers.

That will neither promote the general welfare nor secure any blessings of liberty.

Increasing waves of politicians exalt qualities that should disqualify them as public officials.

If you hate government and you're indifferent to human suffering, you shouldn't run for office. Attacking public education constitutes an attack on our societal fabric.

We need people who believe in government, not hateful bureaucrats eager to scrap crucial institutions people depend on for upward mobility if not basic survival.

It's called "public service" for a reason.

It's called "public service" for a reason.

44/ Death of Kansas Teen Demands Accountability

July 10, 2025

Sedgwick County District Attorney Marc Bennett, who declined to file charges in the death of Cedric Lofton, should face accountability.

Five Sedgwick County Juvenile Intake and Assessment Center officers held a 135-pound, 17-year-old Cedric "C.J." Lofton face down, pressure on his back, until he died in 2021. The Sedgwick County coroner ruled the death a homicide. No one was even arrested, let alone prosecuted.

A panel of U.S. Court of Appeals judges, however, ruled that the detention personnel could not "sidestep an excessive-force lawsuit filed against them," *Kansas Reflector* reported.

Sedgwick County District Attorney Marc Bennett, who declined to charge the detention personnel, should face accountability, too. Prosecutors are the most powerful people in the legal system, yet, like police officers, rarely face the kind of culpability they foist on others.

Kansas Reflector asked Bennett if he had a response, but he declined, saying he could not comment on pending litigation.

The appeals court spoke with the kind of clarity hoped for but missed in the aftermath of Lofton's death. Activists rallied the community. Organizations lent support to groups demanding justice. Gov. Laura Kelly ordered an investigation.

But Bennett didn't budge, arguing, as though he were representing his fellow county government employees, that detention personnel stood immune from prosecution under the state's "robust stand your ground law."

We've seen prosecutors go to great lengths to justify prosecutions, but here, we saw prosecutorial discretion contorting itself like a game of Twister.

The detention officers, Jason Stepien, Brenton Newby, Karen Conklin, William Buckner and Benito Mendoza, should have had to face a judge or jury, but Bennett made the decision that they would not.

Consider these concerning red flags:

1) Detention personnel are law enforcement, and prosecutors tend to maintain cozy relationships with law officers.

2) Lofton was restrained for nearly 45 minutes, roughly 10 minutes longer than Bennett's report noted, according to video footage. One employee restraining Lofton told police he'd applied weight to Lofton's back.

3) Also, according to the *Wichita Eagle*, a former Wichita police officer who changed his answers on a form to leave Lofton at the juvenile lockup where he died had his license revoked.

4) The Kansas Commission on Peace Officers' Standards and Training, which oversees officer certifications, posted the four-page revocation for Ryan O'Hare.

These represent obvious red flags under the standard of avoiding the appearance of impropriety. It felt like a coverup.

Steven Hart, a Chicago-based civil rights attorney representing Lofton's family, told the Eagle the decision not to prosecute was "morally bankrupt."

"Essentially what Marc Bennett is suggesting is, 'You did it to yourself, kid,'" Hart told the *Eagle*.

Hart continued: "You're going to believe on face value what (the county employees) say? Since when has a district attorney said, 'An accused said he didn't do it, so he didn't do it?'"

Sedgwick County District Attorney Marc Bennett, who declined to file charges in the death of Cedric Lofton, should face accountability.

I spoke to Bennett a few weeks ago not only about not prosecuting this case but his more recent decision not to prosecute a young white woman involved in a car accident that killed a young Black man from Emporia.

I asked how he'd respond to suspicions of bias in these cases where young Black people died and no one was prosecuted.

"To compare the two unrelated incidents is baseless," Bennett said. "As was fully explained at the time in a press conference and a report, the decision in the Lofton matter was based on the law of the state of Kansas — to suggest it was because 'less weight' was placed on his life is offensive."

The families missing those young men might find it offensive that no one was held accountable, and frankly, labeling this perspective "baseless" feels cold and dismissive. It also read as though he should not be questioned. Citizens have a duty to question elected officials.

It's important to note that Bennett's no outlier. In our legal system, while district attorneys serve as elected officials, complaints against them tend to land in front of sympathetic panels of former prosecutors.

Kansas Reflector also has followed the shenanigans of Shawnee County District Attorney Mike Kagay, who, despite video evidence to the contrary, emphasized that a man carrying a socket wrench and moving away from officers had charged those officers with a raised knife.

Interestingly, the same lawyer defending those Topeka officers, Jeffrey Kuhlman, represented the juvenile detention officers, too.

An air deficit? You mean suffocation? What a euphemism for homicide.

In 2022, Lofton's brother, Marquan Teetz, filed a federal lawsuit alleging staff used excessive force against Lofton. Kuhlman argued Lofton wouldn't have died had he not resisted in a manner that resulted in exposure to "an air deficit."

An air deficit? You mean suffocation? What a euphemism for homicide.

This ruling offered hope, but our society worships law enforcement, generally refuses to hold officers accountable, and doesn't value the lives of its lower caste. This was clear in Bennett's exoneration of detention personnel and blaming Lofton for struggling to survive.

Donald Black's *The Behavior of Law,* written in 1976, said the offender-victim combination drove decisions. Black argued legal system behavior was "quantifiable, predictable, and follows deducible general rules."

The most prosecuted cases are Black on white crime and white on white crime with white on Black crime and Black on Black crime least prosecuted. Consequently, Lofton's killers likely would escape prosecution.

They should have been prosecuted, and the appeals court seemed to agree.

Court of Appeals Judge Carolyn McHugh, writing for Judges Richard Frederico and Allison Eid of the 10th Circuit, said: "Defendants had sufficient control over (Lofton). At that point, a reasonable officer would have perceived the threat had passed and that the use of deadly force was no longer reasonable. Instead, five officers continued to subject Mr. Lofton to a prone restraint while his legs were restrained, and he appeared not to move for prolonged periods."

This seemed obvious to almost everyone, except Bennett.

45/ Police Seize Student Phones, Passcodes. Parents Cry Foul

December 22, 2025

Police officers turned up at Topeka High School this month and demanded phones and passcodes from multiple students. They didn't notify families before, or after.

Tamika Zollicoffee said her 16-year-old son had never had a run-in with police, but now he may have a record floating in the system because he attended a party near a homicide scene.

Students should not lose their rights when arriving at school, but when police appeared December 8 at Topeka High School with a warrant, they pulled him from class, seized his phone and demanded the passcode.

Zollicoffee said administrators fell short of their duty and that a law enforcement officer abused her son's trust. Her son wasn't alone. The warrant listed the names, race and other personal information of 20 students.

"I felt in my soul that this couldn't be right," she said during a phone interview. "This is so upsetting to me."

The presence of the warrant likely protects police, but repercussions may yet exist for the students. For parents, it appears that police with warrants can question your child at school without notifying you.

Neither the school nor the police department informed her about this incident.

During the public statement portion of a Dec. 16 city council meeting, Zollicoffee expressed frustration with the police department and the school district.

"What happened on Dec. 8th … was totally in my opinion, sloppy, unprofessional and disrespectful to the parents involved," she said, adding later, "The ball was totally dropped, and I feel totally disrespected. (The police) did it behind our backs."

Kansas Reflector contacted the city and the school district for comment. Kimberly Qualls, spokeswoman for the city, said, "Due to the pending judicial process related to the case, the Topeka Police Department is unable to provide additional comment at this time."

The school district did not respond.

Kansas Reflector has not yet seen the warrant.

Lauren Bonds, a civil rights lawyer and executive director of the National Police Accountability Project, said that unfortunately, "there really aren't strong Fourth Amendment protections in cases like this."

While some states have passed protections above those set by courts because of how easily police can coerce students into false confessions and wrongful convictions, Kansas is not among those states, Bonds said.

The warrant gave police cover in this instance, and courts likely would find that school officials had no choice but to comply with police entering the school and waving a warrant.

But that doesn't mean everything that happened was OK.

Bonds said it was reasonable to wonder if being named on a first-degree murder warrant might follow the students around for years. Also, including all the names on one warrant placed students in danger. Again, this was a homicide investigation.

"It's very much a possibility," Bonds said.

She added: "The uncertainty here alone is a problem. It is also imposing a burden. That's incredibly disconcerting."

Zollicoffee feared this.

"The safety of those students was jeopardized," she said. "This could be considered a 'snitch list.'"

Zollicoffee asked the officer she'd tracked down why he would put all the students' names, race and other personal information in one document.

"He said, 'It was easier this way,'" she said.

Tyshika Jones, mother of two students who were questioned, doesn't think so.

"If you would have come and talked to me," Jones said of the police, "I could have told you that my kids didn't even have working phones at the time (of the homicide being investigated). I have receipts and everything."

Jones said the intimidation her daughter faced made matters worse.

"My daughter said she asked three times to speak to me," Jones said. "She kept asking to talk to me, but the officer snatched the phone out of her hand, because she wasn't giving it to him, and told her to 'call her on your own time.'"

Zollicoffee said by not contacting parents, the school district violated its own policy. She quoted 2350-01, the policy that prefers students be questioned outside of business hours and parents to be notified before interrogation.

Parents should have been informed after the questioning as well, Zollicoffee said. That policy has been in place since 1980, and the last revision, she said, was in 2018.

Police attempted to question Jones' son at Eisenhower Middle School, but administrators didn't let the officer question him until they'd notified Jones.

Zollicoffee worries about police digging for new cases against the students as they wander through the confiscated phones.

"Couldn't they just say that they found something and set it aside for a later investigation?" she said.

Zollicoffee worries about police digging for new cases against the students as they wander through the confiscated phones.

She believed race and social class played a role in how police behaved. She said the students seemed to be rounded up like cattle and left alone with police. Almost every student on the list was Black, she said.

"If that was a white school, I don't think they would've walked in, grabbed phones and questioned kids without calling their parents," she said. "We are Black and working class. They just dismissed us."

Had these been white students from wealthy families, she said, "it wouldn't have happened this way. Police would have called and spoken to them and given them the respect they deserved."

She still has not heard from the school system.

46/ Young Republicans' Racist Texts Exposed

November 5, 2025

The bronze statue of Abraham Lincoln on the south lawn of the Kansas Capitol in April 2025. The statue, by Topeka sculptor Merrell Gage, was dedicated in 1918. (Max McCoy/Kansas Reflector)

The issue really isn't the vicious racism in the texts linked to members of the Kansas Young Republicans, exposed by the news website Politico. It's too easy to blame the young adults involved. Sure, they aren't kids. Some have reached 30 and beyond.

Republican adults recently posted culturally insensitive images of Gov. Laura Kelly in a sombrero. The apple, it seems, doesn't fall far from the tree.

The deeper issue is that America needs a healthy Republican Party. It needs the balance. Amid this crisis, the party needs to make a decision: hold to its current, ruinous course, or choose democracy and denounce extremism.

Dithering and rudderless progressives, whose indecision and timidity continue to alienate their party's base, also need work. But we don't see the same kind of virulent racism from Democratic ranks that soaked those text messages. Kansas Young Republicans chair Alex Dwyer and vice chair William Hendrix participated in the Telegram group chat. Hendrix used racial slurs to refer to Black people, including "n–ga" and "n–guh."

In a July conversation on the thread about Black people, Hendrix said, "Bro is at a chicken restaurant ordering his food. Would he like some watermelon and Kool-Aid with that?"

Vice President J.D. Vance has defended the Republican texters, but Kansas Attorney General Kris Kobach fired Hendrix from a communications job as Politico prepared its report.

"The comments in the chat are inexcusable," Kobach said. "As soon as the office learned of those messages, Will Hendrix's employment was terminated."

Dwyer and Hendrix were photographed at a campaign event with Kansas Senate President Ty Masterson, the Andover Republican now running for governor. Masterson denied any connection to the young people beyond the photo.

The text discussion ranged from antisemitism and love for Adolph Hitler to anti-LGBTQ rhetoric. In the chat, Dwyer and others delved into discussions of how GOP operatives could tarnish a political candidate by linking the individual to white supremacists.

Here's the key point.

They dismissed the idea because the plan could backfire in a place such as Kansas, where "Young Republicans could end up becoming attracted to that opponent," Politico wrote.

What a damming admission. These young Republicans considered white supremacy a default belief in parts of the party's base. And these 20- and 30-somethings didn't birth these ideas. The party (and the nation) must come to grips with race instead of trying to bury or to whitewash it. The texts are the result of decades of dalliance with racial invective. Years of "welfare queens," Willie Horton ads, and attacks on civil and voting rights.

Right now, the GOP mourns Charlie Kirk, a man who said: "If I see a Black pilot, I'm going to be like, 'Boy, I hope he's qualified.'"

He also said prominent Black women, including former First Lady Michelle Obama and Supreme Court Justice Ketanji Brown Jackson, who hold multiple Ivy League degrees, "do not have the brain processing power to otherwise be taken really seriously."

These are judgments based only on skin color. President Donald Trump just posthumously awarded Kirk the Presidential Medal of Freedom.

On the chat log, someone was asked to guess what room number they had at a hotel.

Dwyer responded "1488," shorthand among white supremacists when referring to the 14-word, slogan: "We must secure the existence of our people and a future for white children." The "88" stands for "Heil Hitler," with "H" being the eighth letter of the alphabet.

The "states rights" party now wants to occupy the cities of its perceived political opponents over the objections of governors.

Today's Republican Party bears little resemblance to the party President Abraham Lincoln led. Once Democratic President Lyndon Johnson passed the Civil Rights Act in 1964, the parties essentially switched jerseys. Since then, the GOP generally has opposed civil rights and voting rights. Still, conservatism has long meant limited government, individual freedom, the rule of law and a belief in an enduring moral order.

I'm told that my great-grandfather, as was true with many Black people before Kennedy, was a proud Republican, still honoring Lincoln's efforts to end slavery.

There are many proud moments from a healthier time for the modern version of the party.

President Dwight D. Eisenhower sent the 101st Airborne into Little Rock to enforce the *Brown v. Board* decision. He desegregated Washington, D.C., and federal bases. He tried to keep segregationists off the federal bench, if you believe Ike biographer David Nichols. A Republican judge Ike appointed in Alabama, Frank Minis Johnson, lifted an injunction that allowed the Rev. Martin Luther King Jr.'s voting rights march to proceed. Arizona U.S. Sen. Barry Goldwater walked into the White House and told President Richard Nixon, amid Watergate, that the time had come for Nixon to step down.

But there's nothing conservative about exploding the debt. The current administration campaigned on free speech yet has targeted comedians for mocking the president and his cabinet. The "states' rights" party now wants to occupy the cities of its perceived political opponents over the objection of governors.

That's a very unhealthy position.

Republicans' ability to reconnect with proud moments of their past would bode well for their future — and for the nation's.

47/ Kansas Magistrate Gets Smart on Bail Bonds

September 4, 2025

Ron Sylvester, a retired magistrate judge, says bail bonds are unnecessary in most nonviolent cases. Text messages have proven sufficient to get people to return to court.

Magistrate Judge Ron Sylvester's story about the need to eliminate cash bonds in nonviolent cases begins with two QuikTrip hot dogs, one actual dog, and a man with mental health and addiction issues struggling to survive.

Setting bonds, said Sylvester, who retired in April after five years on the bench, doesn't protect communities. It can, however, mock justice as it did for a then-74-year-old Thomas Wimberly, who spent 71 days in jail for stealing hot dogs he gave to his dog, Smokey Bear.

Retired Magistrate Judge Ron Sylvester (Kansas Judicial Branch)

Bail bonds, in Sylvester's estimation, are regressive, exploitative legal system versions of payday loans that prey on people like Wimberly. Sylvester, a journalist for 40 years who covered courts for the Wichita Eagle, shared a story he'd written almost 20 years ago.

It was early July in 2006 when Wimberly put Smokey Bear into a shopping cart and headed to a downtown Wichita car show. On the way home, he stopped at a QuikTrip and grabbed two hot dogs for the hungry Smokey Bear.

But as Wimberly prepared the last hot dog, he saw Smokey Bear climbing out of the cart and left the store without paying. A moonlighting police officer saw Wimberly leave without paying the $2.11 he owed.

By the time the officer reached Wimberly, Smokey Bear had gulped the hot dogs.

Wimberly was booked on theft but his case was dismissed.

Sylvester said Wimberly thought it was over. Not close.

Wimberly had two previous misdemeanor thefts on his record — one more than a decade old. This third misdemeanor became a felony under Kansas law. The city sent the case to the district attorney's office.

The summons the D.A.'s office sent to attend a hearing came back undelivered. So, when Wimberly didn't show, a judge issued a bench warrant that sent Wimberly to jail on what for him was a whopping $5,000 bond.

Sylvester said bail bond services typically post a bond for 10% of the amount, but $500 exceeded what Wimberly drew in a month from Social Security. At the time of his arrest, Wimberly lived on $448 a month.

Jurors took two days off work when the case went to trial. They heard the evidence and found Wimberly not guilty. Sylvester said some jurors were irate the case went to trial.

"It was stupid," presiding juror Krysti Mason, 21, said of Wimbley's trial in the Eagle article

With the national conversation now about cracking down on crime, it isn't wrong to wonder where this narrative that the nation is soft on crime comes from. Our nation has 5% of the world's population but 25% of its criminals. We *are* tough on crime.

It's time we got smart on crime. At roughly $50 a day for 71 days, the system spent a minimum of $3,550 on Wimberly's $2.11 hot dog heist.

Sylvester said Wimberly, who also suffered from mental health issues, got Smokey Bear back and that Wimberly often carried the newspaper story with him, basking in his 15 minutes of fame.

Wimberly has since died, but his story and the cruel system of bail bonds live on.

The bonds are unnecessary, Sylvester said of most nonviolent cases. Text messages have proven sufficient to get people to return to court. The bond industry, he said, preys on fear, claiming bond-less defendants would be dangers to the community.

"Yeah, with them on the mean streets of Kingman, we aren't safe," he said sarcastically of the south-central Kansas town where he served as a magistrate. "All (the current system) does is allow rich, dangerous people to roam the community."

Sylvester often offered defendants "OR bonds," or own recognizance bonds. Defendants paid only if they didn't show up for court dates. Besides, most of the people who appeared in front of him needed help, not punishment.

"About 90 to 95% of the cases I heard had a mental health or addiction component or both," he said. "A lot of this has to do with the failure to pass Medicaid."

He appeared in a Wall Street Journal article about Pratt Regional Medical Center suing many of its patients because it was the only way to generate the revenue necessary to keep the hospital open.

> *"All (the current system) does is allow rich, dangerous people to roam the community."*

The Journal featured Sylvester in a story last year about how 95% of the civil cases he was hearing were brought by the hospital. In July and August 2023, four of every five sheriff-delivered court summonses in Pratt County were from the hospital.

"By December," the story said, "it had sued some 400 people in a county of 9,000 — more than it had in the past five years combined."

Sylvester said people who appeared in front of him pleaded for help.

"I've told anyone who would listen that if you want to be tough on crime, you should work to properly fund community mental health and addiction treatments in every Kansas town. You do that, and you will significantly cut crime, especially in rural areas."

And maybe not spend thousands of dollars on bonds and hot dog larceny.

48/ We Must Look Out for One Another to Prosper

October 9, 2025

The Rev. Martin Luther King Jr. once said that as long as poverty existed, he could never be rich, even with a billion dollars.

"As long as diseases are rampant and millions of people in this world cannot expect to live more than 28 or 30 years, I can never be totally healthy even if I just got a good checkup at Mayo Clinic," he said. "I can never be what I ought to be until you are what you ought to be."

King saw stunning inequality some 60 years ago and proposed structural changes to help make the country whole. These ideas — the death of inequality and the survival of a common good — could determine society's future.

Some 27,000 Kansans lost Supplemental Nutrition Assistance Program access after passage earlier this summer of President Donald Trump's H.R. 1 bill that shifted millions in federal responsibilities to states.

This vast new wave of food insecurity could create another social pathogen.

Back in 2016, a Clemson University researcher offered "An Examination of Food Insecurity and Its Impact on Violent Crime in American Communities." The study, by Jonathan Randel Caughron, "examines how the relationship between food insecurity and violent crime varies in relation to the level of dependent variables such as the income level and population level of the county."

The study suggested a 1% increase in food insecurity could lead to a 12% increase in violent crime.

Mean policy — cutting access to food and education — seems to produce mean people. We are more connected than many care to admit, no matter how many walls and gated communities we build. We fixate on symptoms but avoid causes.

This nation remains proficient at tough and even cruel anti-crime measures. Consider what this portends, especially as inequality continues to rise. According to an Associated Press article from 2019, U.S. inequality had grown to its highest level in a half-century. Yes, it said, "even in Kansas."

"The gap between the haves and have-nots in the United States grew last year to its highest level in more than 50 years of tracking income inequality, according to U.S. Census Bureau," the article said.

It went on: "Income inequality in the United States expanded from 2017 to 2018, with several heartland states (like Kansas and Nebraska) among the leaders of the increase, even though several wealthy coastal states still had the most inequality overall."

The report noted that not only had Kansas opted to not raise the minimum wage, but the economic recovery also led to windfalls for those owning "stocks, property, and other assets."

The article referenced University of Kansas economist Donna Ginther, who said: "The winners tend to be at the top. Even though we are at full employment, wages really haven't gone up much in the recovery."

There remains a school of thought that poverty reflects bad choices and bad character. Even King reportedly exhorted Black Americans to prepare themselves for full citizenship by getting their financial houses in order.

But he also said: "The curse of poverty has no justification in our age. The time has come for us to civilize ourselves by the total, direct, and immediate abolition of poverty."

King spoke often of the systems that support a culture of poverty.

"True compassion," he said, "is more than flinging a coin to a beggar; it is not haphazard and superficial. It comes to see that an edifice which produces beggars needs restructuring."

And: "One day we must ask the question, 'Why are there 40 million poor people in America?' And when you begin to ask that question, you are raising questions about the economic system, about a broader distribution of wealth."

Extremists frequently quote King out of context about "content of character," and "color of skin," but they never acknowledge his commitment to the poor, a belief system that likely got King killed.

King objected to the war in Vietnam, arguing that military spending drained resources for "social uplift" programs.

"The bombs in Vietnam explode at home; they destroy the hopes and possibilities for a decent America," he said.

King wasn't alone. President Dwight Eisenhower expressed similar thoughts.

"Every gun that is made, every warship launched, every rocket fired signifies, in the final sense, a theft from those who hunger and are not fed, those who are cold and not clothed," he said. "This world in

We are more connected than many care to admit, no matter how many walls and gated communities we build.

arms is not spending money alone. It is spending the sweat of its laborers, the genius of its scientists, the hopes of its children."

Ike sounds like King there. The question becomes just how this "Christian" nation will respond. What does this mean for wealthy Christians seemingly choosing a third or fourth house and a fourth or fifth car over food and shelter for suffering people?

H.R. 1, also called the "big, beautiful bill," represented to many observers the greatest transfer of wealth from the poor and working class to the wealthy in the nation's history. But people are not disposable, and we are not meant to live in isolation.

"This is the way our world is made," King said. "No individual or nation can stand out boasting of being independent. We are *interdependent*."

49/ Some 68 Years after *Brown v. Board*, Similar Foes

May 15, 2022

A tour group observes the Brown v. Board **mural on the third floor of the Kansas Statehouse on April 26, 2022. (Sherman Smith/Kansas Reflector)**

During a 2014 symposium marking the 60th anniversary of the *Brown v. Topeka Board of Education* decision, a statement from one of the plaintiffs offered what today feels like prescient insight. [Five cases from Kansas, Delaware, South Carolina, D.C., and Virginia were combined in the case named *Brown.*] Many of the Virginia plaintiffs in the class-action lawsuit feared integration and would have preferred separate and *actually* equal.

Many historians consider *Brown* one of the high court's five most consequential decisions. The landmark ruling struck down 1896's *Plessy v.*

Ferguson ruling solidifying segregation in schools and the concept of "separate but equal." Nevertheless, the opposition has persisted.

As we approach *Brown*'s 72nd birthday, and the seating of the Supreme Court's first female African American jurist, much of this age-old fight feels so familiar.

For many, the decision remains a proud moment for the nation, a moment where America not only aligned itself with its soaring egalitarian narrative, but where it also acknowledged a tragic failing it had long tried to keep hidden.

According to a news release about the symposium, convened at the University of Kansas, "in addition to establishing integration in public schools, the case was a significant step toward changing a broader dynamic of discrimination in the years and decades that followed. The ruling revolutionized the legal framework for race relations, extended the protection of equal rights to all and inspired oppressed peoples around the world to become advocates of freedom and equality."

Langston Hughes once wrote, "America has never been America to me," but for a fleeting moment, many in Black America thought America might finally "be" for them.

But that moment proved short-lived.

Symposium presenter Hasan Kwame Jeffries, an associate professor of history at The Ohio State University argued that society had underestimated segregationist resolve, pointing to a dedicated, three-pronged resistance movement that included grassroots protests, legal filings and the establishment of private schools.

> *"Either the United States will destroy ignorance, or ignorance will destroy the United States."*
> ~W. E. B. DuBois

Theodore Shaw, the former head of the NAACP Legal Defense Fund, referred to *Brown* during his remarks at the symposium as "Hallowed, but hollow," and said New York City schools were as segregated today as they were before Brown.

But then, there was John Stokes, one of the Virginia plaintiffs.

He explained to me and my son, whom I'd brought along, that Virginia plaintiffs made up 75 percent of the Brown plaintiffs and many of them, himself included, simply wanted school officials to honor their promise of "equal" schools.

Mr. Stokes said he knew the white, Southern, often government-sanctioned terror that marked the era would collapse on them as soon as they attempted to enter the schools. The thought of that terrified him, he said.

In our society, white resistance is regarded by many as patriotic (Jan. 6, for example).

Mr. Stokes did not underestimate the resolve. He'd seen it up close.

For many the decision remains a proud moment for the nation.

Consider the continuing hysterical claims that school officials have embedded Critical Race Theory (a graduate-level study) in grade school curriculums, that diversity makes white children feel bad, and that certain books should be pulled from library shelves.

Proponents of these breathless claims have leveled violent threats at school board members, school administrators and classroom teachers nationwide.

Meanwhile, white flight into wealthy suburbs created homogeneous neighborhoods with housing costs beyond the means of most Black families, meaning schools there will resemble the neighborhoods. The spread of private, Christian schools invulnerable to Constitutional appeals to equality has continued.

All this, while claiming a wholesome innocence.

This year, according to The Grio website, of the 47 senators voting against Ketanji Brown Jackson's appointment to the Supreme Court, 25 had voted for her less than a year ago for lower judicial positions. South Carolina Sen. Lindsey Graham had voted for her twice.

Jackson will have to wait until late June or early July to take her seat, but she'll land on a court seemingly more hostile to civil rights and civil liberties than the Earl Warren-led Court that handed down the Brown decision almost seven decades ago.

Things have changed somewhat, but this environment still feels so familiar.

Noted scholar W.E.B. DuBois once said, "Either the United States will destroy ignorance or ignorance will destroy the United States." After decades of running and with many decades to go, not only have we not pulled away from ignorance, we're still running neck-and-neck.

50/ Million Man March Still Inspires

November 12, 2025 published in the *Missouri Independent*

Million Man March (Million Man March Facebook page)

For many of the men who caravanned for hours in buses and cars to Washington, D.C., for the October 16, 1995 Million Man March, the event marked an attempt toward a modern Harlem Renaissance, also known as "the New Negro Movement."

The 1990s produced new grotesqueries like the criminological theory of "super predators," a small but growing population of Black youths supposedly committing violent acts without remorse. They joined the absent father and the incorrigible criminal in urban lore.

The nation ignored the swaths of Black men who tried lifting their quiet lives above the noisy images.

Thirty years ago this month, many of these upright men booked trips to D.C. in hopes of changing a narrative so powerful that despite their lives of uplift, doubt often overshadowed their belief in themselves.

Nation of Islam leader Louis Farrakhan conceived the march, but Christian organizers helped. The event drew Christian men with little knowledge of Islam. I covered the event for the *Wichita Eagle*, following a group of local men making the voyage. They seemed cautiously optimistic that they would make history and introduce their true selves to the nation, and there on the National Mall, they found safe harbor.

An entire day free of the hideous images that had long defined them.

Literary icon Maya Angelou offered a poignant new etching of Black men with a verse from her "Million Man March Poem," saying: "I look through the posture and past your disguise / And see your love for family in your big brown eyes."

Rosa Parks, whose refusal to move from her seat on a city bus in Montgomery, Alabama, and who helped move segregation off its axis 1955, spoke. So did Martin Luther King III, some 27 years after his father's towering words elevated civil rights to a moral endeavor. A boy with an afro and wearing a daishiki spoke powerfully, as did representatives from Africa and the Caribbean. Ivy League professor Cornel West also spoke.

The program lasted for more than 12 hours and included pledges of personal responsibility, protecting women and children, and building and supporting Black businesses back home.

The event likely remains the largest gathering of Black men in the history of this nation, a day of affirmation that inspired future President Barack Obama as well as generations of community advocates and political officials.

Professor Ron Walters, a native Wichitan and architect of the Congressional Black Caucus, attended and sat with event dignitaries.

"The real test of the success of this march is going to be what the people do when they get home," said Walters, then the head of Howard University's political science department, to CNN.

Nearly two million African American men registered to vote the year after the march.

Washington, D.C., authorities recorded no acts of violence, drunkenness, drugs, physical fights or acts of destruction. The love and brotherhood on the mall that day overwhelmed many of the participants, surpassing their fondest hopes.

Leaving, however, meant a return to the usual.

It began for a Wichita contingent the morning after the march. The bus buzzed about the experience. The men regarded the trip as a pilgrimage to self-acceptance and as a pivotal moment in their lives. But stopping in Ohio for a newspaper, eager to see their historic day memorialized, the gleeful chatter slid into silence as paper after paper reported a crowd of 400,000. A subsequent study by Boston University placed the count between 670,000 and 1.1 million, but the initial count took some sheen off the event.

The low count plunged participants into the lives they had before the trip, but this felt different. The march had given them jolts of resolve. Undaunted, they returned to their communities. They joined existing organizations and started new ones. Nearly 2 million African American men registered to vote the year after the march.

Memories of the march linger, but under layers of time, like smudges on a nearly forgotten hand mirror.

The shiny image from that day slumbers under the years, but with scrubbing, the person we always knew existed surfaces again, gazing at us with big, brown eyes.

51/ Boots on the Ground

I'm here today, to ask you to **swim.** You'll understand better in a moment.

Mark Twain said history doesn't necessarily repeat itself, but it does rhyme.

We're in a new period of Retrenchment, similar to post Reconstruction, similar to the post Civil Rights movement, and now, following the historic presidency of Barack Obama. According to the National Urban League, we are in **a state of emergency.**

Some 300,000 Black women and counting have lost their jobs this year.

Neo-Nazis and other hate groups are now marching with arrogance.

We are facing direct attacks on our jobs, our history, and our institutions. There are escalating efforts to dismantle voting rights; to block access to fair elections; to erode gains fought for over generations.

Democracy, civil rights and **progress itself**, face tireless attacks.

People in masks are snatching people off the street. Racial profiling now seems legal. Due process seemingly has been annulled.

It's bleak.

And yet...

In many ways, we've been here before, and we survived.

Today reminds me of the great Bill Withers who once sang:

> *When the day that lies ahead of*
> *me, seems impossible to face.*
>
> *And when someone else instead of me,*
>
> *always seems to know the way...*
>
> *Then I look at you.*
>
> *And the world's alright with me.*
>
> *Just one look at you.*
>
> *And I know it's going to be*
>
> *A lovely day...*

Your presence here today is **political speech**. It is an assertion of your willingness to put in the work. It's an indication that you have not given up on democracy. It means that you're determined to not only rescue our nation from this era of retrenchment, but to drive the moorings deeper and to build the spires higher for the continued ascendancy of this multi-racial democracy.

Give yourself a hand for your courage.

I read a tremendous book earlier this year titled "The Barn: The Secret History of a Murder in Mississippi" by author Wright Thompson. It details the torture and murder of young Emmett Till in the barn where his killers actually took **water breaks** between sessions of beating him.

The author, a Southern white man born and raised near that barn, was interviewed on one of the morning news shows a couple of weeks ago. He said two things that resonated powerfully with me.

First, when asked about reactions to his book, he said his readers uniformly say that those who now control government "want a return to a **pre-civil rights America."**

Second, he said he was standing on the banks of the Tallahatchie River in Mississippi with the niece of Mose Wright, Emmett Till's uncle from whose house Till was kidnapped.

In that moment of quiet, he asked Mr. Wright's niece: "What are you thinking about while you're standing here?" "What are you feeling?"

Breaking the silence she said, "I'm just so grateful."

Stunned, Thompson said he didn't understand.

She then said, "because he got out of the river," and Thompson said it clicked for him.

You see, the Tallahatchie is called the "singing river" because of all the lynched bodies that had been tossed into it. It's as though those bodies will forever cry out for justice.

"Yeah," she said, "I'm so glad he got out."

Young Emmett Till, he didn't find justice for himself. But he did help create justice for millions of people he didn't know and never met.

That's important, Thompson said because there are so many people who want to put Till **back** in the river **along with decades of civil rights advances.**

They want to submerge all that history. To erase it from memory.

Our opponents, as a strategy, attack what they perceive as our greatest strength: a history of resistance and resilience – thus the attacks on history and on museums.

It's a "**tell**." What they **attack** most, is what they most **fear**.

They want that history, and all the remedies created because of it, back on the bottom of the Tallahatchie river.

Right now, we must be willing to sacrifice for gains we may never see, for people we don't even know.

True generosity, is planting a tree whose shade you'll never get to experience. People in the Civil Rights Movement faced firehoses – with streams at 100 lbs. per square inch, powerful enough to break ribs and rip hair from the scalp – because they wanted something better for the next generation.

My friend Judy Sheery said, "I'm not mad at the single mom working three jobs for not being here today. She's trying to survive."

"But," Judy said, "We need to help her. We have a responsibility to her."

This is why, I'm asking you to **swim**. This is why we **need** you to swim.

Swim to the banks, all of you, and increase our numbers and raise our voices.

Swim out to those floating, blissfully unaware, and lead them to shore and into this movement.

Swim to those who are drowning and drag them to shore.

Swim to groups like Boots on the Ground Midwest, and give them your time, your talent, or your treasure. Not everybody can give the **same** thing, but we can all give **something**.

We know you may have to swim through some stiff currents trying to pull you under. We know the water is murky and cold. We realize it's a long distance.

But **swim**. Swim as hard as you can.

Get out of the river.

Before our Democracy sinks.

About the Author

Mark McCormick is a *New York Times* best-selling author with nearly thirty years of experience as a reporter, editor, and columnist. He was appointed by Kansas governor Laura Kelly to two state commissions and is a trustee of the William Allen White School of Journalism at the University of Kansas. He was inaugural director of the Kansas Black Leadership Council and has earned numerous other awards and recognitions during his career, including, in 2025, being inducted into the Kansas Press Association's Newspaper Hall of Fame.

This is Mark McCormick's third book. His others are: *Bye Bye Barry* (written with Barry Sanders) and *Some Were Paupers, Some Were Kings: Dispatches from Kansas*. Mark is also much in demand as a speaker.

Mark grew up in Wichita and graduated from the University of Kansas School of Journalism. For five years he was on the staff of the Louisville, Kentucky's *Courier-Journal*. For nearly fourteen years he was an editor and columnist at the *Wichita Eagle*. He subsequently spent time in the nonprofit sector, including six years as Executive Director of the Kansas African American Museum. He also served as communications director and deputy director of the ACLU of Kansas. Currently he is a Fellow at the Dole Institute of Politics at the University of Kansas and opinion writer for the *Kansas Reflector*.

"Mark ... watches this state and its people with a keen eye and big heart. He speaks out for the little guy. And he doesn't put up with any nonsense from those in power," says Clay Wirestone of the *Reflector.* "Talking to Mark makes me feel smarter and better informed. He thinks deeply, and his wisdom serves as a guidepost to the rest of us."

Mark McCormick